THE VANISHING HITCHHIKER

Also by Jan Harold Brunvand

THE STUDY OF AMERICAN FOLKLORE: AN INTRODUCTION
(Second Edition)

READINGS IN AMERICAN FOLKLORE

The Vanishing Hitchhiker

American Urban Legends and Their Meanings

JAN HAROLD BRUNVAND

UNIVERSITY OF UTAH

W · W · NORTON & COMPANY
New York   London

Published simultaneously in Canada by
George J. McLeod Limited, Toronto

Printed in the United States of America

Library of Congress Cataloging in Publication Data
Brunvand, Jan Harold.
THE VANISHING HITCHHIKER:
American urban legends and their meanings
1. Legends—United States. 2. Cities and
towns (in religion, folklore, etc.)—United
States. I. Title.
GR105.B69   1981   398.2′09173′2   81–4744
ISBN 0–393–01473–8   AACR2
ISBN 0–393–95169–3 (pbk.)

W. W. Norton & Company, Inc.
500 Fifth Avenue, New York, N.Y. 10110
W. W. Norton & Company Ltd.
25 New Street Square, London EC4A 3NT

2 3 4 5 6 7 8 9 0

To my students
past and present
believers and skeptics alike

Contents

Contents

Contents

CHAPTER 6—DALLIANCE, NUDITY, AND NIGHTMARES

CHAPTER 7—BUSINESS RIPOFFS: TWO FAVORITE MEDIA LEGENDS

CHAPTER 8—URBAN LEGENDS IN THE MAKING

Contents

Preface

This is a book about modern American folk narratives, stories
that most people have heard as true accounts of real-life experiences, and few except scholars recognize as an authentic
and characteristic part of our contemporary folklore. Folklorists
—specialists in the collection and analysis of such traditions—
refer to these believable stories about vanishing hitchhikers,
batter-fried rats, grandmothers' runaway corpses and the like as
"urban belief tales" or, simply, "urban legends."

The juxtaposition of the terms "modern," "contemporary,"
and "urban" and the word "folklore" may seem contradictory to
those who think of folklore as charming, obsolete, unsophisti-
cated traditions passed along by wheezing old gaffers and
cackling crones in the backwoods villages of bygone days.
Urban legends, on the contrary, are realistic stories concerning recent events (or alleged events) with an ironic or supernatural twist. They are an integral part of white Anglo-Ameri-
can culture and are told and believed by some of the most
sophisticated "folk" of modern society—young people, urbanites,
and the well educated. The storytellers assume that the true
facts of each case lie just one or two informants back down
the line with a reliable witness, or in a news media report.

mass media

The mass media themselves participate in the dissemination and apparent validation of urban legends, just as they sometimes do with rumor and gossip, adding to their plausibility. But, as this book demonstrates, urban legends are folklore, not history.

In common with age-old folk legends about lost mines, buried treasure, omens, ghosts, and Robin Hood-like outlaw heroes, urban legends are told seriously, circulate largely by word of mouth, are generally anonymous, and vary constantly in particular details from one telling to another, while always preserving a central core of traditional elements or "motifs." To

"motifs"

some degree—again like much other folklore—urban legends must be considered *false,* at least in the sense that the same rather bizarre events could not actually have happened in so many localities to so many aunts, cousins, neighbors, in-laws, and classmates of the hundreds and thousands of individual tellers of the tales. Both the narrative structure of these legends and their characteristic traditional folk motifs and oral variations disqualify them as literal accounts of actual events. The Hook Man's lane is a real locale in numerous communities, and a solid cement Cadillac has been reported "reliably" more than once—even photographed—but the myriad re-tellings and re-localizations (sometimes internationally) of these stories reveal beyond a doubt that they are simply additional instances of our living folklore. Still, like traditional folklore, the stories do tell one kind of truth. They are a unique, unselfconscious reflection of major concerns of individuals in the societies in which the legends circulate.

It is not the purpose of folklore study to debunk oral traditions, although it may seem so to those who may have asked a folklorist about "The Death Car" or "Red Velvet Cake" only to learn that another favorite story has supposedly happened many times before to scores of other people. For a folklorist, collecting a story's variations and tracing its dissemination and change through time and space are only the beginning of an analysis. We may or may not discover an original mouse tail

Preface

in a pop bottle or a spider in a hairdo, but the wide distribution and acceptance of these and other similar traditions teach us something about how Americans react to situations involving corporate or individual negligence of health and cleanliness standards. *Why* these stories are told is our major concern. The lessons in the mouse tail or spider legend could just as well have been promoted by means of a factory inspector's directive, but the interesting fact is that the attitudes are much more graphically and memorably conveyed among the folk by these strange, believable, false-true tales.

American folklorists have collected and published a considerable number of urban legend texts and produced a few notable studies of their variation and distribution. A great many more texts of urban legends are filed in folklore archives or are simply in individual folklorists' notes. Interpretations of these traditional cultural materials are still rather scarce, however. This book brings together scholars' findings on some of the best known American urban legends, along with further materials from my own files and my students' papers, and suggests the larger patterns and possible meanings of these contemporary folk narratives. Of course there are possible reflections of much older motifs in some of the new legends, and finding these to analyze their psychological significance would be most interesting, but such speculation is beyond the scope of this book.

Since many of my examples come from Indiana, where numerous urban legends have been collected and studied in the Indiana University folklore program, and from Utah, where I teach, the distribution patterns indicated here are somewhat skewed. But the legends are truly national, often international, and the number of examples and variety of details could easily be expanded at least tenfold by the addition of the legend texts stored in other folklore archives and private collections. My purpose is to be broadly representative rather than definitive, since a complete study of any single urban legend could easily take a book of its own. Several of these legends are the subjects of ongoing professional studies, and wherever possible I have referred to conference papers and other unpublished material kindly made available to me by other scholars. Many urban legends have inspired popular printed, filmed, or televised plots, but a thorough and systematic review of this aspect is beyond the scope of this study. (A few such offshoots are mentioned in the notes.)

In addition to the articles and books cited in the notes and my own students' work, identified wherever quoted, a number of individuals supplied me with extra information or helped to locate obscure sources. These debts are acknowledged individually in the notes, but I wish to express my deep and sincere thanks again to the following people: Louie Attebery, Ron Baker, Mac Barrick, Betty Jane Belanus, Frances Borden and Lola Preiss (of the Waldorf-Astoria), Dick Bothwell (of the *St. Petersburg Times*), Meg Brady, Tom Burnam, George Carey, Bill Clements, Bob Cochran, Loren Coleman, Keith Cunningham, Gary Alan Fine, Lydia Fish, Peter Goss, Sylvia Ann Grider, Sandy Ives, Bill McNeil, Donna Lou Morgan (of the *Salt Lake Tribune*), Lynn Packer (of KSL-TV), Sharon Pratt, Sue Samuelson, Cynthia Scheer, Mike and Dew Shonsey, Dave Stanley, Bob Steensma, and Bert Wilson.

An extract from this book appeared under the title "Urban Legends: Folklore for Today" in *Psychology Today*, 14:1 (June 1980), 50–62.

THE VANISHING HITCHHIKER

1 New Legends for Old

process of legend formation (handwritten)

We are not aware of our own folklore any more than we are of the grammatical rules of our language. When we follow the ancient practice of informally transmitting "lore"—wisdom, knowledge, or accepted modes of behavior—by word of mouth and customary example from person to person, we do not concentrate on the form or content of our folklore; instead, we simply listen to information that others tell us and then pass it on—more or less accurately—to other listeners. In this stream of unselfconscious oral tradition the information that acquires a clear story line is called *narrative folklore*, and those stories alleged to be true are *legends.* This, in broad summary, is the typical process of legend formation and transmission as it has existed from time immemorial and continues to operate today. It works about the same way whether the legendary plot concerns a dragon in a cave or a mouse in a Coke bottle.

It might seem unlikely that legends—*urban* legends at that —would continue to be created in an age of widespread literacy, rapid mass communications, and restless travel. While our pioneer ancestors may have had to rely heavily on oral traditions to pass the news along about changing events and frontier dangers, surely we no longer need mere "folk" reports of what's happening, with all their tendencies to distort the

1

facts. A moment's reflection, however, reminds us of the many weird, fascinating, but unverified rumors and tales that so frequently come to our ears—killers and madmen on the loose, shocking or funny personal experiences, unsafe manufactured products, and many other unexplained mysteries of daily life. Sometimes we encounter different oral versions of such stories, and on occasion we may read about similar events in newspapers or magazines; but seldom do we find, or even seek after, reliable documentation. The lack of verification in no way diminishes the appeal urban legends have for us. We enjoy them merely as stories, and we tend at least to half-believe them as possibly accurate reports. And the legends we tell, as with any folklore, reflect many of the hopes, fears, and anxieties of our time. In short, legends are definitely part of our modern folklore—legends which are as traditional, variable, and functional as those of the past.

def. folklore

Folklore study consists of collecting, classifying, and interpreting in their full cultural context the many products of everyday human interaction that have acquired a somewhat stable underlying form and that are passed traditionally from person to person, group to group, and generation to generation. Legend study is a most revealing area of such research because the stories that people believe to be true hold an important place in their worldview. "If it's true, it's important" is an axiom to be trusted, whether or not the lore really *is* true or not. Simply becoming aware of this modern folklore which we all possess to some degree is a revelation in itself, but going beyond this to compare the tales, isolate their consistent themes, and relate them to the rest of the culture can yield rich insights into the state of our current civilization. Such is the premise of this book, and from it derives the method which it follows.

Urban Legends as Folklore

Folklore subsists on oral tradition, but not all oral communication is folklore. The vast amounts of human interchange, from casual daily conversations to formal discussions in business or industry, law, or teaching, rarely constitute straight oral folklore. However, all such "communicative events" (as scholars dub them) are punctuated routinely by various units of traditional material that are memorable, repeatable, and that fit recurring social situations well enough to serve in place of original remarks. "Tradition" is the key idea that links together such utterances as nicknames, proverbs, greeting and leave-taking formulas, wisecracks, anecdotes, and jokes as "folklore"; indeed, these are a few of the best known "conversational genres" of American folklore. Longer and more complex folk forms—fairy tales, epics, myths, legends, or ballads, for example—may thrive only in certain special situations of oral transmission. All true folklore ultimately depends upon continued oral dissemination, usually within fairly homogeneous "folk groups," and upon the retention through time of internal patterns and motifs that become traditional in the oral exchanges. The corollary of this rule of stability in oral tradition is that all items of folklore, while retaining a fixed central core, are constantly changing as they are transmitted, so as to create countless "variants" differing in length, detail, style, and performance technique. Folklore, in short, consists of oral tradition in variants.

Urban legends belong to the subclass of folk narratives, legends, that—unlike fairy tales—are believed, or at least believable, and that—unlike myths—are set in the recent past and involve normal human beings rather than ancient gods or demigods. Legends are folk history, or rather quasi-history. As with any folk legends, urban legends gain credibility from specific details of time and place or from references to source authorities. For instance, a popular western pioneer legend often begins something like, "My great-grandmother had this strange experience when she was a young girl on a wagon train going through Wyoming when an Indian chief wanted to adopt her . . ." Even though hundreds of different great-grandmothers are supposed to have had the same doubtful experience (being

3

desired by the chief because of her beautiful long blond hair), the fact seldom reaches legend-tellers; if it does, they assume that the family lore has indeed spread far and wide. This particular popular tradition, known as "Goldilocks on the Oregon Trail," interests folklorists because of the racist implications of a dark Indian savage coveting a fair young civilized woman—this legend is familiar in the *white* folklore only— and it is of little concern that the story seems to be entirely apocryphal.

In the world of modern urban legends there is usually no geographical or generational gap between teller and event. The story is *true;* it really occurred, and recently, and always to someone else who is quite close to the narrator, or at least "a friend of a friend." Urban legends are told both in the course of casual conversations and in such special situations as campfires, slumber parties, and college dormitory bull sessions. The legends' physical settings are often close by, real, and sometimes even locally renowned for other such happenings. Though the characters in the stories are usually nameless, they are true-to-life examples of the kind of people the narrators and their audience know firsthand.

One of the great mysteries of folklore research is where oral traditions originate and who invents them. One might expect that at least in modern folklore we could come up with answers to such questions, but this is seldom, if ever, the case. As is shown in subsequent chapters, most leads pointing to possible authors or original events lying behind urban legends have simply evaporated.

The Performance of Legends

Whatever the origins of urban legends, their dissemination is no mystery. The tales have traveled far and wide, and have been told and retold from person to person in the same manner that myths, fairy tales, or ballads spread in earlier cultures, with the important difference that today's legends are also disseminated by the mass media. Groups of age-mates, especially adolescents, are one important American legend channel, but other paths of transmission are among office workers and club members, as well as among religious, recreational, and regional groups. Some individuals make a point of learning every recent rumor or tale, and they can enliven any coffee break, party, or trip with the latest supposed "news." The telling of one story inspires other people to share what they have read or heard, and in a short time a lively exchange of details occurs and perhaps new variants are created.

Tellers of these legends, of course, are seldom aware of their roles as "performers of folklore." The conscious purpose of this kind of storytelling is to convey a true event, and only incidentally to entertain an audience. Nevertheless, the speaker's demeanor is carefully orchestrated, and his or her delivery is low-key and soft-sell. With subtle gestures, eye movements, and vocal inflections the stories are made dramatic, pointed, and suspenseful. But, just as with jokes, some can tell them and some can't. Passive tellers of urban legends may just report them as odd rumors, but the more active legend tellers re-create them as dramatic stories of suspense and, perhaps, humor.

"The Boyfriend's Death"

With all these points in mind about folklore's subject-matter, style, and oral performance, consider this typical version of a well-known urban legend that folklorists have named "The Boyfriend's Death," collected in 1964 (the earliest documented instance of the story) by folklorist Daniel R. Barnes from an eighteen-year-old freshman at the University of Kansas. The usual tellers of the story are adolescents, and the normal setting for the narration is a college dormitory room with fellow students sprawled on the furniture and floors.

Stable elements
variable traits

THE VANISHING HITCHHIKER

This happened just a few years ago out on the road that
turns off 59 highway by the Holiday Inn. This couple
were parked under a tree out on this road. Well, it got to
be time for the girl to be back at the dorm, so she told
her boyfriend that they should start back. But the car
wouldn't start, so he told her to lock herself in the car and
he would go down to the Holiday Inn and call for help.
Well, he didn't come back and he didn't come back, and
pretty soon she started hearing a scratching noise on the
roof of the car. "Scratch, scratch . . . scratch, scratch." She
got scareder and scareder, but he didn't come back. Finally,
when it was almost daylight, some people came along and
stopped and helped her out of the car, and she looked up
and there was her boyfriend hanging from the tree, and
his feet were scraping against the roof of the car. This is
why the road is called "Hangman's Road."

Here is a story that has traveled rapidly to reach nationwide
oral circulation, in the process becoming structured in the
typical manner of folk narratives. The traditional and fairly
stable elements are the parked couple, the abandoned girl, the
mysterious scratching (sometimes joined by a dripping sound
and ghostly shadows on the windshield), the daybreak rescue,
and the horrible climax. Variable traits are the precise location, the reason for her abandonment, the nature of the rescuers, murder details, and the concluding placename explanation. While "The Boyfriend's Death" seems to have captured
teenagers' imaginations as a separate legend only since the
early 1960s, it is clearly related to at least two older yarns,
"The Hook" and "The Roommate's Death" (discussed in Chapter 3). All three legends have been widely collected by American folklorists, although only scattered examples have been
published, mostly in professional journals. Examination of some
of these variations helps to make clear the status of the story
as folklore and its possible meanings.

At Indiana University, a leading American center of folklore
research, folk-narrative specialist Linda Dégh and her students

6

have gathered voluminous data on urban legends, especially those popular with adolescents. Dégh's preliminary published report on "The Boyfriend's Death" concerned nineteen texts collected from IU students from 1964 to 1968. Several story-tellers had heard it in high school, often at parties; others had picked it up in college dormitories or elsewhere on campus. Several students expressed some belief in the legend, supposing either that it had happened in their own hometowns, or possibly in other states, once as far distant as "a remote part of Alabama." One informant reported that "she had been sworn to that the incident actually happened," but another, who had heard some variations of the tale, felt that "it seemed too horrible to be true." Some versions had incorporated motifs from other popular teenage horror legends or local ghost stories; one text evidently drew some influence from the urban legend "The Runaway Grandmother," since the characters are "a lady and her husband . . . driving in the desert of New Mexico" (see Chapter 5).

One of the Indiana texts, told in the state of Washington, localizes the story there near Moses Lake, "in the country on a road that leads to a dead-end right under a big weeping willow tree . . . about four or five miles from town." As in most American versions of the story, these specific local touches make believable what is essentially a traveling legend. In a detail familiar from other variants of "The Boyfriend's Death," the body—now decapitated—is left hanging upside down from a branch of the willow tree with the fingernails scraping the top of the car. Another version studied by the Indiana researcher is somewhat aberrant, perhaps because the student was told the story by a friend's parents who claimed that "it happened a long time ago, probably thirty or forty years." Here a murderer is introduced, a "crazy old lady" on whose property the couple has parked. The victim this time is skinned rather than decapitated, and his head scrapes the car as the corpse swings to and fro in the breezy night.

A developing motif in "The Boyfriend's Death" is the character and role of the rescuers, who in the 1964 Kansas version are merely "some people." The standard identification later becomes "the police," authority figures whose presence lends further credence to the story. They are either called by the missing teenagers' parents, or simply appear on the scene in the morning to check the car. In a 1969 variant from Leonardtown, Maryland, the police give a warning, "Miss, please get out of the car and walk to the police car with us, but don't look back." (Concerning the murderer, this storyteller added, "Everyone supposed it was the Hook Man who had done this"; again, see Chapter 3.) In a version from Texas collected in 1971, set "at this lake somewhere way out in nowhere," a policeman gets an even longer line: "Young lady, we want you to get out of the car and come with us. Whatever you do, don't turn, don't turn around, just keep walking, just keep going straight and don't look back at the car." The more detailed the police instructions are, the more plausible the tale seems to become. Of course the standard rule of folk-narrative plot development now applies: the taboo must be broken (or the "interdiction violated," as some scholars put it). The girl always *does* look back, like Orpheus in the underworld, and in a number of versions her hair turns white from the shock of what she sees, as in a dozen other American legends.

In a Canadian version of "The Boyfriend's Death," told by a fourteen-year-old boy from Willowdale, Ontario, in 1973, the words of the policemen are merely summarized, but the opening scene of the legend is developed more fully, with several special details, including one usually found in the legend "The Hook"—a warning heard on the car radio. The girl's behavior when left behind is also described in more detail.

> A guy and his girlfriend are on the way to a party when their car starts to give them some trouble. At that same time they catch a news flash on the radio warning all people in the area that a lunatic killer has escaped from a local criminal asylum. The girl becomes very upset and at that point the car stalls completely on the highway. The

boyfriend gets out and tinkers around with the engine but can't get the car to start again. He decides that he is going to have to walk on up the road to a gas station and get a tow truck but wants his girlfriend to stay behind in the car. She is frightened and pleads with him to take her, but he says that she'll be safe on the floor of the car covered with a blanket so that anyone passing will think it is an abandoned car and not bother her. Besides he can sprint along the road and get back more quickly than if she comes with him in her high-heeled shoes and evening dress. She finally agrees and he tells her not to come out unless she hears his signal of three knocks on the window. . .

She does hear knocks on the car, but they continue eerily beyond three; the sound is later explained as the shoes of the boyfriend's corpse bumping the car as the body swings from a limb above the car.

The style in which oral narratives are told deserves attention, for the live telling that is dramatic, fluid, and often quite gripping in actual folk performance before a sympathetic audience may seem stiff, repetitious, and awkward on the printed page. Lacking in all our examples of "The Boyfriend's Death" is the essential ingredient of immediate context—the setting of the legend-telling, the storyteller's vocal and facial expression and gestures, the audience's reaction, and the texts of other similar tales narrated at the same session. Several of the informants explained that the story was told to them in spooky situations, late at night, near a cemetery, out camping, or even "while on a hayride or out parked," occasionally near the site of the supposed murder. Some students refer to such macabre legends, therefore, as "scary stories," "screamers," or "horrors."

A widely-distributed folk legend of this kind as it travels in oral tradition acquires a good deal of its credibility and effect from the localized details inserted by individual tellers. The highway and motel identifications in the Kansas text are good examples of this, and in a New Orleans version, "The Boyfriend's Death" is absorbed into a local teenage tradition about

"The Grunch"—a half-sheep, half-human monster that haunts specific local sites. One teenager there reported, "A man and lady went out by the lake and in the morning they found 'em hanging upside down on a tree and they said grunches did it." Finally, rumors or news stories about missing persons or violent crimes (as mentioned in the Canadian version) can merge with urban legends, helping to support their air of truth, or giving them renewed circulation after a period of less frequent occurrence.

Even the bare printed texts retain some earmarks of effective oral tradition. Witness in the Kansas text the artful use of repetition (typical of folk narrative style): "Well, he didn't come back and he didn't come back. . . . but he didn't come back." The repeated use of "well" and the building of lengthy sentences with "and" are other hallmarks of oral style which give the narrator complete control over his performance, tending to squeeze out interruptions or prevent lapses in attention among the listeners. The scene that is set for the incident— lonely road, night, a tree looming over the car, out of gas— and the sound effects—scratches or bumps on the car—contribute to the style, as does the dramatic part played by the policeman and the abrupt ending line: "She looked back, and she saw. . . . !" Since the typical narrators and auditors of "The Boyfriend's Death" themselves like to "park" and may have been alarmed by rumors, strange sights and noises, or automobile emergencies (all intensified in their effects by the audience's knowing other parking legends), the abrupt, unresolved ending leaves open the possibilities of what "really happened."

Urban Legends as Cultural Symbols

Legends can survive in our culture as living narrative folklore if they contain three essential elements: a strong basic story-appeal, a foundation in actual belief, and a meaningful message or "moral." That is, popular stories like "The Boy-

3 elements
① strong story appeal
② foundation in actual belief
③ a meaningful message a moral

friend's Death" are not only engrossing tales, but also "true,"
or at least so people think, and they teach valuable lessons.
Jokes are a living part of oral tradition, despite being fictional
and often silly, because of their humor, brevity, and snappy
punch lines, but legends are by nature longer, slower, and more
serious. Since more effort is needed to tell and appreciate a
legend than a joke, it needs more than just verbal art to carry
it along. Jokes have significant "messages" too, but these tend to
be disguised or implied. People tell jokes primarily for amusement, and they seldom sense their underlying themes. In legends the primary messages are quite clear and straightforward;
often they take the form of explicit warnings or good examples
of "poetic justice." Secondary messages in urban legends tend to
be suggested metaphorically or symbolically; these may provide
deeper criticisms of human behavior or social conditions.

People still tell legends, therefore, and other folk take time
to listen to them, not only because of their inherent plot interest
but because they seem to convey true, worthwhile, and relevant
information, albeit partly in a subconscious mode. In other
words, such stories are "news" presented to us in an attractive
way, with hints of larger meanings. Without this multiple appeal few legends would get a hearing in the modern world,
so filled with other distractions. Legends survive by being as
lively and "factual" as the television evening news, and, like
the daily news broadcasts, they tend to concern deaths, injuries, kidnappings, tragedies, and scandals. Apparently the
basic human need for meaningful personal contact cannot be
entirely replaced by the mass media and popular culture. A
portion of our interest in what is occurring in the world must
be filled by some face-to-face reports from other human beings.

On a literal level a story like "The Boyfriend's Death" simply
warns young people to avoid situations in which they may be
endangered, but at a more symbolic level the story reveals
society's broader fears of people, especially women and the
young, being alone and among strangers in the darkened world
outside the security of their own home or car. Note that the

young woman in the story (characterized by "her high-heeled shoes and evening dress") is shown as especially helpless and passive, cowering under the blanket in the car until she is rescued by men. Such themes recur in various forms in many other popular urban legends, as we shall see.

In order to be retained in a culture, any form of folklore must fill some genuine need, whether this be the need for an entertaining escape from reality, or a desire to validate by anecdotal examples some of the culture's ideals and institutions. For legends in general, a major function has always been the attempt to explain unusual and supernatural happenings in the natural world. To some degree this remains a purpose for urban legends, but their more common role nowadays seems to be to show that the prosaic contemporary scene is capable of producing shocking or amazing occurrences which may actually have happened to friends or to near-acquaintances but which are nevertheless explainable in some reasonably logical terms. On the one hand we want our factual lore to inspire awe, and at the same time we wish to have the most fantastic tales include at least the hint of a rational explanation and perhaps even a conclusion. Thus an escaped lunatic, a possibly *real* character, not a fantastic invader from outer space or Frankenstein's monster, is said to be responsible for the atrocities committed in the gruesome tales that teenagers tell. As sometimes happens in real life, the car radio gives warning, and the police get the situation back under control. (The policemen's role, in fact, becomes larger and more commanding as the story grows in oral tradition.) Only when the young lovers are still alone and scared are they vulnerable, but society's adults and guardians come to their rescue presently.

In common with brief unverified reports ("rumors"), to which they are often closely related, urban legends gratify our desire to know about and to try to understand bizarre, frightening, and potentially dangerous or embarrassing events that *may* have happened. (In rumors and legends there is always some element of doubt concerning where and when these things *did* occur.) These floating stories appeal to our morbid curiosity and satisfy our sensation-seeking minds that demand gratification through frequent infusions of new information, "sanitized" somewhat by the positive messages. Informal rumors and stories fill in the gaps left by professional news reporting, and these marvelous, though generally false, "true" tales may be said to be carrying the folk-news—along with some editorial matter—from person to person even in today's highly technological world.

Interpreting Urban Legends

Collections of verbatim oral texts from their natural contexts, along with background information about storytellers and their listeners, are the basis for reliable interpretations of folk stories' meanings and functions in the societies in which they are found. Texts from the mass media need to be identified by date and place of publication as well as to their likely audiences. Insofar as possible, the history and distribution of any given tale should be made clear from the collected examples of it. Unfortunately, these ideals were not always met in past folk-narrative studies, but it should be the goal of all present and future collectors to secure the fullest possible data on stories and their human sources. For urban legends this ought to become standard procedure, since they belong to an ongoing tradition that is easily observed.

Even with incomplete data, some worthwhile conclusions about the meanings of urban legend are possible when the existing information is evaluated and compared. Folklorists assume that no cultural data is devoid of meaning, and that any data from a culture may cast some light on the meaning of other data from the same culture. A few observations about the folkloristic methods of analysis applicable to urban legend research are in order before giving further examples.

As already noted, in any living oral tradition, such as storytelling, certain stable elements persist at the same time that other elements are in constant variation. By the process sometimes referred to as "communal re-creation," people in a folk community absorb new material into their oral culture, then remake it through repetition and creative retelling. The resulting oral narratives are somewhat stereotyped and formalized in broad terms, but also they are always fluid and changing in details. The first step in identifying and classifying an oral-narrative tradition such as that of an urban legend is to distinguish the stable elements from the variable units.

For the purpose of study, the stable parts of urban legends are usually stated as generalized descriptions of basic stages in the plot, such as the couple parking, the threat from outside, the rescue, and the final revelation of the crime in "The Boyfriend's Death." These abstracted actions are then compared to the story units of other traditional legends (as shown in later chapters), and their underlying structural patterns described. Often, for example, sets of opposites dominate urban legend plots; these may be expressed in such paired terms as old/young, life/death, home/away, good/bad, reality/fantasy, and the like. Another typical pattern, common in many kinds of folk narratives, is threefold repetition, with the climax at the third stage. In these repeated standardized patterns of oral tradition we find solid clues as to the meanings stories convey, whether explicitly as straightforward warnings, or less directly in symbolic form.

Like other narrative folklore, urban legends develop two kinds of variations. Many changes are predictable adaptations to make the stories fit local conditions. Especially in an oral tradition that is considered true (like legends), circumstantial details of name, place, time, and situation often enter into narrators' performances. More significant variations, however, go beyond local color to introduce new characters, objects, or plot elements, and especially attempts on the part of storytellers to explain the story (sometimes called "oral-literary criticism"). When other narrators repeat and expand upon these variable elements, they become accepted into a wider tradition and further shape legends as cultural symbols. In "The Boyfriend's Death," for example, we saw how the details of the girl's reaction to stress and the enlargement of the policemen's part in the story both reflect how American society expects young women and authority figures to behave in times of crisis. Comparative folklore research has also shown us how such older traditional "motifs"—individual plot elements—as violation of a taboo ("Don't look back!") and hair turning white from fear became attached to this newer legend. (Traditional narrative motifs have been cataloged in Stith Thompson's six-volume standard reference work *The Motif-Index of Folk-Literature*. Gathering similar motifs from widespread traditions is the first step in assessing the historical, and possible psychological, connections between different folk cultures, a task for which this book provides raw material concerning urban legends.)

Along with material from the urban legend tradition itself, other social and cultural aspects of modern life related to the subject matter of legends are considered in an interpretation. Folklorists ask what else the culture says about the same subjects in expressive forms other than folklore. Evidence may be sought in popular culture, institutions (such as school and church), patterns of family life, social interaction, and the like. What are the standards of behavior that the characters in legends either conform to or disregard? Do the messages of legends support or attack society's expectations?

Perhaps the most telling aspect of legend interpretation—but often the most lacking in past collections—is solid information about the narration of legends in their natural contexts. What little we know about *who* tells the stories, *when, to whom,* and *why* invariably contributes towards understanding how legends function and what they mean. Too frequently, however, our contextual and background information is limited to the name, age, sex, and address of informants; seldom do we find scholarly studies that give close descriptions of actual storytelling events. As a result, we must make the best of what we have (as this book attempts to do) and we must encourage

context

the further study of urban legends in much more depth and with better social, cultural, and performance data. Some specific guidelines towards this end are contained in the Appendix.

The following chapters examine the best known and most characteristic American urban legends, tracing in oral and published versions their spread and variation, and asking frequently "*Why* are these stories told so avidly?" and "What do they mean?" For convenience of discussion the legends have been grouped thematically, but the reader should bear in mind that meanings are multiple in any folklore, and so these categories are never mutually exclusive. Furthermore, your own oral versions of urban legends are every bit as "authentic" as those previously collected by folklore scholars; after all, *you* are the folk who possess and transmit this genre of modern folklore.

NOTES

The Kansas version of "The Boyfriend's Death" comes from Daniel R. Barnes's article "Some Functional Horror Stories on the Kansas University Campus," *Southern Folklore Quarterly*, 30 (1966), 309–310. Linda Dégh's discussion of the story is in the excellent regional journal she edits in Bloomington, Indiana, titled *Indiana Folklore*, which has been largely devoted to publishing legend texts and studies since its founding. "The Boyfriend's Death" is in volume 1 (1968), pp. 101–106. The Maryland version is from George Carey's article "Some Thoughts on the Modern Legend," in the *Journal of the Folklore Society of Greater Washington* [D.C.], vol. 2, no. 1 (Winter, 1970–71), p. 8, an article which was reprinted with several additions in Carey's book *Maryland Folk Legends and Folk Songs* (Cambridge, Maryland: Tidewater Publishers, 1971), pp. 79–80. Danielle Roemer included the Texas example in her fine analytical article "Scary Story Legends" published in the University of Texas graduate student publication *Folklore Annual,* no. 3 (Austin, 1971), pp. 1–16 (story on pp. 12–13). The Canadian story was collected by Susan Smith, a York University student, from a teenager in Toronto in 1973 and published in Edith Fowke's *Folklore of Canada* (Toronto: McClelland and Stewart, 1976), pp. 263–264. For the New Orleans tradition see Kristie Harling, "The Grunch: An Example of New Orleans Teen-Age Folklore," *Louisiana Folklore Miscellany,* vol. 3, no. 2 (April, 1971), pp. 15–20.

Patrick B. Mullen's article "Modern Legend and Rumor Theory," *Journal of the Folklore Institute,* 9 (1972), 95–109, is a very useful survey of approaches to studying rumors, and it includes references to several urban legends. Two important articles on mass media and modern folklore are contained in vol. 40 of *Southern Folklore Quarterly;* they are Donald Allport Bird's "A Theory for Folklore in Mass Media: Traditional Patterns in the Mass Media" (pp. 285–305), and Ronald L. Baker's "The Influence of Mass Culture on Modern Legends" (pp. 367–376). Rosan Jordan deCaro documented the spread of rumors via mass media—specifically in the newspaper advice columns—in her essay "Sex Education and the Horrible Example Stories" in *Folklore Forum,* 3 (1970), 124–127.

Larry Danielson compared 143 "stories about apparition visitations" from oral tradition and mass media sources by means of statistical analysis of length, content elements, structure, and style in his article "Toward the Analysis of Vernacular Texts," *Journal of the Folklore Institute,* 16 (1979), 130–154. Danielson's prefatory comments concern various media versions of "The Vanishing Hitchhiker" (see Chapter 2).

Texts of nine urban legends (six coming from *Indiana Folklore*) were reprinted in Duncan Emrich's *Folklore on the American Land* (Boston: Little, Brown, 1972), pp. 327–338. Tom Burnam's book *More Misinformation* (New York: Lippincott & Crowell, 1980) refers to a number of urban legends under the heading "Folk Myths and Fantasies," on pages 83–97. Dick Bothwell, columnist for the *St. Petersburg* [Florida] *Times,* frequently publishes urban legends, about a dozen of which are included in reprinted columns compiled as *BUM (Brighten Up Monday) Stories* (St. Petersburg: Great Outdoors Publishing Co., 1978).

The Swedish folklorist Bengt af Klintberg documented the characteristic elements of a number of urban legends found in his country in an article titled "Folksägner i dag" [Folk Legends Today] in the journal *Fataburen* (1976), 269–296.

2 | The Classic Automobile Legends

As tellers of American urban legends, whether adolescents or adults, we are a highly mobile and often fairly affluent folk, so it is natural that many of our favorite plots involve private cars and public highways. Earlier generations told more stories of haunted houses, hunting adventures, or witchcraft, but we prefer stories centering on the family automobile, pleasure trips, and the open road.

The role of the automobile in many well-known urban legends is significant. Access to a car allows youngsters to separate themselves from family, home, and even from the inhibiting company of peers (except for a date or a close friend) for a considerable period of time. For a lower- or middle-class family a car provides a temporary escape from the humdrum world of home, neighborhood, or suburb. Americans' growing fascination with cars and increased ownership of them, especially since World War II, has had a tremendous effect not only on social customs and mores but also on modern folklore. A good example of the strong desire to own a car is evident in "The Death Car," a classic automobile legend that has been repeatedly updated since the late 1930s and fed both by rumor and the mass media. This brief version is from a student paper in one of my own folklore classes in 1969:

"The Death Car"

My friend from Los Angeles breathlessly announced that she could pick up a $5,400 Porsche Targa sports car for only $500. The reason for the reduced price was that it had sat in the middle of the Mojave Desert for one week with a dead man in it; consequently, the smell of death could not be removed from it.

This is the bare-bones story with these recurrent motifs: expensive car, low price, suicide or murder, corpse long undiscovered, and lingering smell of death. Other students in my class told me it was a Ford Thunderbird, an MG, or "a 1971 Corvette selling for $75 and advertised in a Boise, Idaho, newspaper." Richard M. Dorson has written, reporting a typical experience of many folklorists, "Every folklore class I have taught [at Michigan State University] contained students who knew and believed this story." Dorson was able to date it in Michigan, where the car is usually a Buick or a Cadillac, first back to 1944 as an anonymous legend, then trace it to the small central Michigan black community of Mecosta as a firsthand report of an event that occurred there in 1938 involving known named individuals, a suicide undiscovered for three months, and a distinctively decorated 1929 Ford. He compared all the data and concluded that "unlikely as it seems" this must have been the origin of the ubiquitous "Death Car" legend.

In an article titled "The Folklore of the Motor-car" University of Leeds (England) folklorist Stewart Sanderson summarized a British version, "The Ineradicable Blood-Stain"; the car, stained by the owner's blood when he committed suicide, is sold "for a nominal sum" by the widow. The tale, Sanderson reports, is known from 1951 onwards in various parts of England.

"The Death Car" often appears more like a rumor—an unstructured, unverified, anonymous oral or published report—

than a legend—a complete, well-rounded, "true" story circulating in oral tradition. In fact, "The Death Car" tends to pop up now and then, proliferating rumorlike for a few weeks or months before fading out for another dormant period. Probably the story is especially popular with younger narrators (although plenty of adults know it too) because of the tantalizing motif of getting something for next to nothing. The price tag on the car, incidentally, has kept up with inflation, going roughly from $50 in the 1940s to about $500 in the 1960s and 1970s. The tendency to flesh out the rumor to a full-scale story with a particular message of local significance is illustrated in this University of Maryland student's version, which concludes with an expression of dislike for a specific car dealer who was supposedly involved:

> You know that car dealer out on University Boulevard? Its specialty is repossessed cars. Well, they say they repossessed this red Corvette a few years ago. The owner had been murdered and hidden in the trunk. Well, this car dealer cleaned up the car, repainted it and re-carpeted the trunk, and about a week later they sold that car to some guy. But he returned the car after a week, said there was a bad smell in it that he couldn't get rid of. This happened a couple of more times with other people who bought the car, and now that dealer is stuck with the car. I think its going price is something like $100. But it serves them right. That place is a big clip joint anyway. I hope they never sell the car.

The status of such urban legends as folklore is unquestionable, despite the common belief among tellers and listeners that they are truthful accounts, or at least are based on actual events. The amazing thing is that so few people seem to encounter enough variants of the stories to question them, or if they do, they fail to perceive that multiple, varying texts in oral tradition are good evidence against credibility. It is also surprising that few individuals, other than occasional folklorists or journalists, become curious enough about the alleged first-hand sources of the stories to follow the leads back a few steps to the—inevitable—dead end. (Dorson reported that Lansing, Michigan, Buick dealers were flooded with calls about the non-existent inexpensive smelly car. Did the dealers never pass these stories on to the callers and debunk the tradition, or *can* such legends ever be put down?) The explanation for this situation lies, I think, mainly in the nature of folklore. First, it is simply traditional to listen to and appreciate a good story without undue questioning of its premises. Second, "belief" in an item of folklore is not of the same kind as believing the earth is round or that gravity exists. A "true story" is first and foremost a story, not an axiom of science. And third, the legends fulfill needs of warning (don't park!), explanation (what may happen to those who do), and rationalization (you can't really expect sensational bargains not to have strings attached); these needs transcend any need to know the absolute truth. The appeal and durability of a superb morbid mystery tale is as strong in folklore as in fiction or film, and the significance of a "folk" telling of such events can be as great for a scholar as its appearance in a popular-culture medium or in literature.

"The Philanderer's Porsche"

Since "The Death Car" itself never seems to turn up for sale—and the smell of death seems quite tolerable to the would-be sports car owner—may we not trust in the slightly less astonishing but still fully believable tale, "The Philanderer's Porsche"? Ann Landers published this hoary story in 1979, sent in to her by a faithful reader who claimed to have read it in the *Chicago Tribune*:

> A man in California saw an ad in the paper for an "almost new" Porsche, in excellent condition—price $50. He was certain the printers had made a typographical error,

but even at $5,000 it would have been a bargain, so he hurried to the address to look at the car.

A nice-looking woman appeared at the front door. Yes, she had placed the ad. The price was indeed $50. "The car," she said, "is in the garage. Come and look at it."

The fellow was overwhelmed. It was a beautiful Porsche, and, as the ad promised, "nearly new." He asked if he could drive the car around the block. The woman said, "Of course," and went with him.

The Porsche drove like a dream. The young man peeled off $50 and handed it over, somewhat sheepishly. The woman gave him the necessary papers, and the car was his.

Finally, the new owner couldn't stand it any longer. He had to know why the woman was selling the Porsche at such a ridiculously low price. Her reply was simple: With a half-smile on her face, she said, "My husband ran off with his secretary a few days ago and left a note instructing me to sell the car and the house, and send him the money."

Ann Landers, always trusting in human nature and in her research contacts, accepted the story as a true one and asked the *Tribune* managing editor about it: "He, too, had read the story and thought it was hilarious," Ann reported, "but his researchers could not find it in their paper. However, the incident did happen as reported and was a news story somewhere."

Now think about it: would a man who is going off with his secretary not do it in his Porsche (possibly one reason she fell for him to start with), and would he really trust his poor abandoned wife to dispose of his property fairly? Not surprisingly, we find that essentially the same story sometimes concludes in other versions with the wife saying that she was merely carrying out her late husband's instructions in his will that she sell the car and give the proceeds to his mistress. This form of the story has been known in England since 1948 and was reprinted in the press there as recently as 1969. Both treatments of the theme—philanderer's expensive car sold cheaply by irate wife (or widow)—dramatize the undeniable pleasure of "getting even."

Roadside Ghosts: "The Vanishing Hitchhiker"

A prime example of the adaptability of older legends is "The Vanishing Hitchhiker"—*the* classic automobile legend. This returning-ghost tale was known by the turn of the century both in the United States and abroad. It acquired the newer automobile motif by the period of the Great Depression, and thereafter spawned a number of subtypes with greatly varied and oddly interlocking details, some of which themselves stemmed from earlier folk legends. Merely sampling some of the many "Vanishing Hitchhiker" variants that have been collected over a period of some forty years can help us trace the legend's incredible development. Surely most readers already know a local "true" account (or maybe two or three) similar to Example A, as told by a teenager in Toronto, Canada, in 1973:

A

Well, this happened to one of my girlfriend's best friends and her father. They were driving along a country road on their way home from the cottage when they saw a young girl hitchhiking. They stopped and picked her up and she got in the back seat. She told the girl and her father that she just lived in the house about five miles up the road. She didn't say anything after that but just turned to watch out the window. When the father saw the house, he drove up to it and turned around to tell the girl they had arrived—but she wasn't there! Both he and his daughter were really mystified and decided to knock on the door and tell the people what had happened. They told them that they had once had a daughter who answered the description of the girl they supposedly had picked up, but she had disappeared some years ago and had last been seen hitchhiking on this very road. Today would have been her birthday.

This version has the basic elements—not necessarily "original" ones—well known in oral tradition and occasionally reported in newspapers since the early 1930s. The stable story units have been labeled in brackets in the following text from South Carolina collected by workers of the South Carolina Writers' Project (Work Projects Administration) sometime between 1935 and 1941:

B

A traveling man [driver] who lived in Spartanburg [authentication] was on his way home one night [setting] when he saw a woman walking along the side of the road [hitchhiker]. He stopped his car and asked the woman if he could take her where she was going. She stated that she was on her way to visit her brother who lived about three miles further on the same road [her address]. He asked her to get in the car and sit by him, but she said she would sit in the back of the car [her choice of seat]. Conversation took place for a while as they rode along, but soon the woman grew quiet. The man drove on until he reached the home of the woman's brother, whom he knew [more authentication]; then stopped his car to let the woman alight. When he looked behind him, there was no one in the car [disappearance]. He thought that rather strange [curiosity or concern], so went into the house and informed the brother that a lady had gotten into his car to ride to see him, but when he arrived at the house the lady had disappeared. The brother was not alarmed at all and stated that the lady was his sister who had died two years before [identification]. He said that this traveling man was the seventh to pick up his sister on the road to visit him, but that she had never reached his house yet.

Variations on the basic story are endless, and trying to sort them out into any kind of possible chronological development is hampered by the fact that the date when a version happened to be collected and published bears little relationship to its possible age in tradition, and by the principle that legends become highly localized and rationalized with many circumstantial details whenever they are adopted into a particular context. For instance, the plot has several different twists and turns in this 1935 version (paraphrased by the collector) from Berkeley, California:

C

This story was heard in a Durant Avenue boarding house, told several times as a true story. It happened to a friend of the narrator. This friend was driving up Hearst Avenue one rainy night. As he came to North Gate (Hearst and Euclid avenues) he saw a girl, a student with books under her arm, waiting for the streetcar. Since these had stopped running, he offered her a ride. She lived up on Euclid. They drove out along Euclid quite a way with some conversation. As they were crossing an intersection, another car came down the steep hill and they would have crashed if the girl had not pulled on the emergency brake [a unique detail in the story]. The fellow was flabbergasted and sat looking at the other car, which pulled around him and went on. When he remembered his companion and looked over, she was gone. Since it was near her home, he assumed she had simply gotten out to walk the rest of the way; but she had left a book on the seat. The next day he went to return the book. He found her father, an English professor, at home. He said that the girl was his daughter, that she had been killed in an auto accident at the same corner one or two years ago that very day. But since the fellow had the book, the father took it into the library, to look on the shelves for it—he found the place where it should have been vacant.

A strictly urban setting for the story allows for more precise and thorough double-checking of factual details. In 1941 Rosalie Hankey of the University of California, who was gathering materials for a lengthy study of "The Vanishing Hitchhiker," tried to verify specific accident reports from Berkeley. In one version the automobile crash in which the girl was killed was supposed to have happened in 1935 or 1936 at the corner of College and Bancroft. But in checking the Berkeley city records from 1934 to 1937, Hankey found that only a single accident involving personal injury, non-fatal, had occurred at that corner during the five-year period.

The specific "proof" in the story of the hitchhiker's actual presence in the car and her status as the ghost of a particular individual is always a key motif. Besides the book she leaves behind in Example C, the object may be a purse, a suitcase, a blanket, a sweater, a scarf or some other item of clothing, or simply footprints or water spots in the car. The identification of her at the family's home may depend upon showing the object to her relatives, or upon the driver's description of her, the girl's name, or a photograph of her which is displayed on the piano or mantel and which often shows her wearing the same party dress in which her ghost appears. One group of variants which includes either the clothing (hers or something borrowed from the driver) or the portrait detail (sometimes both) moves the climax of the story to a cemetery. Also, as in this example from Los Angeles (1940), the pickup in these variants is often made at a club or dance rather than along a street or highway:

D

This actually happened to a fellow I know. He and his friend were in a beer joint in downtown Los Angeles. They met a young woman there. She asked them if they'd take her home because she lived in the same neighborhood (Belvedere Gardens). So they all got in the car and she sat in the back seat. It was a very cold night and she borrowed one of their overcoats. When they

27

reached the Evergreen Cemetery, she asked them if they'd stop a minute. So they stopped and let her out. They waited. When she didn't come back they thought she had stolen the overcoat. They got a little aggravated and went out to look for her. They went into the cemetery and looked around. Then they saw the overcoat draped over a headstone.

(Most versions incorporating the borrowed coat, or sweater, motif improve upon the climax by first establishing through a conversation at her home who she is and when she died. Example D, however, does suggest to us the interesting possibility of hitchhiking-ghost hoaxes, based on the plot of the popular urban legend.)

"Vanishing Hitchhiker" stories involving the portrait-identification motif frequently take a couple of other characteristic turns. The driver may be a cab driver and his passenger a nun who delivers a prophetic message—albeit an unreliable one—before evaporating from the back seat. This example comes from Chicago, December 1941:

E

This mysterious story went the rounds here last winter, and I first heard it from "a friend who heard it from a friend in Chicago who had heard it from her neighbor."

Mike, the cab driver, tells this story of a mysterious fare he had in early December. Cruising on a street in downtown Chicago he picked up an elderly Sister of some Catholic order and was told to take her to _____ Street. He had his radio on and they talked about Pearl Harbor for a while. She said, "It won't last more than four months." Then they drove on and Mike drew up at the address. Jumping out to open the cab door he was surprised to find no one there. Afraid the little old lady "jumped" her fare he hastened to inquire at the address. It was a convent and when questioned by the Superior in charge Mike told of the Sister who had disappeared and hadn't paid her fare. "What did she look like?" the Superior asked, and explained that no Sister from the convent had been downtown that day. As Mike described her, he happened to look at a picture hanging on the wall behind the Superior's desk. "That's her," Mike said, and thought to himself that he would get the fare after all. But the Mother Superior smiled quietly and said, "But she has been dead for ten years."

In a San Francisco variation of the tale collected the following year the cab driver recognizes his passenger in a "life-size statue of the Blessed Virgin," while in some Kingston, New York versions the passenger was identified as Mother Cabrini, the first American citizen canonized as a Catholic saint.

About eight years earlier, versions of the "prophesying passenger" subtype of the legend associated with the Century of Progress Exposition of 1933–1934 appeared in the Chicago area. This one, from Joliet, Illinois, 1933, is typical:

F

People in an automobile going to the Century of Progress Exposition in Chicago are hailed by a woman with a traveling bag, standing by the roadside. They invite her to ride and she gets into the car, but her face is dark and they are unable to see it clearly. She gets into conversation and tells them that the fair in Chicago is going to slide off into Lake Michigan in September. She gives them her address in Chicago and invites them to call there. When they turn around to speak to her, they cannot find her; she has disappeared. They go to the address and meet a man; usually it is the woman's husband. After he has heard the story he says, "Yes, that was my wife. She died four years ago."

Again proving folklore's constant variability, the prophesying passenger tale acquired a new and more accurate form of "proof" which has been dubbed "the corpse in the car." And, as this typical report published in the *San Francisco Chronicle* (January 26, 1942) shows, the vanishing motif then itself vanishes from the story. (Another possibility is that "The Corpse in the Car" is a separate legend which has merged with "The Vanishing Hitchhiker.")

G

Bluffton, Ind., Jan. 25. Mrs. Robert Nuddin of Elwood, Ind., related this story here today: She and her husband, driving to Indianapolis to visit her sister, Mrs. August Leimgruber, saw an old man walking along the road and gave him a ride. "I have no money to pay for your kindness," he said as he left the car. "But I can answer any question you may wish to ask." Nuddin asked when the war would end. "That's easy," said the man. "It will end in July." The Nuddins laughed but the hitchhiker repeated his prediction and said it would come true as surely "as you will have a dead man in your car before you reach home."

Near Indianapolis an ambulance passed the Nuddin car, skidded and overturned in a ditch. The driver asked Nuddin to take the patient to a hospital in Indianapolis. The patient was dead on arrival.

"The Vanishing Hitchhiker" is unusual among urban legends in deriving from earlier supernatural folk legends with foreign antecedents. Many ghosts, in fact, are said to be on endless quests—such as The Flying Dutchman's—for peace and contentment back home. Folklorist Louis C. Jones established this link to traditional ghostlore by citing a number of New York state versions—some of them associated with European immigrant storytellers—reliably dated to the late nineteenth century and involving travelers on horseback. Here is one of his examples:

H

(Collected by Catherine S. Martin, 1943, from her mother Grace C. Martin, who lived as a girl in and near Delmar, a small town, eight miles southwest of Albany, New York, The story was current in the 1890's.)

Mother has told of tales that she has heard of a ghost rider who used to jump on young men's horses as they went past a certain woods near Delmar on their way to parties. The rider, a woman, always disappeared when they arrived at their destination. She was believed to have been a jealous one, but did little harm except riding behind the young man.

A long, artistically told, and highly detailed version of this same legend was collected in Mountain Home, Arkansas, by Vance Randolph in 1941 (credited as being current "about 1930"). Here the girl rides double behind a young man, holding on to him and breathing against his neck. She says her name is Lucy and asks to dismount a short distance before her home near a small country cemetery. The young man rides on to her home, eats supper with her father, Judge Stapleton, and this is the description of their conversation the next morning:

I

. . . the Judge says him and his wife just moved here a year ago. "We used to live two miles down the road," he says, "but our house was lightnin'-struck and burnt plumb down. There ain't nothing left now but the old chimney." The traveler says Yes, he seen that chimney when he rode by there last night. [It was the spot where he picked up Lucy.] "I didn't mind losing the house," says the Judge, "only our daughter was sick in bed. We carried her out to the gate, but the shock was too much for her, and she died that same night."

The fellow just set there, and the Judge went on

a-talking about what a fine girl his daughter was, and how him and the old woman was pretty lonesome nowadays. "We buried her in that little graveyard," says the Judge. "You can see her stone from the front gallery. There ain't a day goes by, rain or shine, that my wife don't walk over there and set by the grave awhile."

Everything was mighty still for a minute, and then the traveler says: "What was your daughter's name?" It sounded kind of funny the way he said it, but he was obliged to know.

"Her name was Lucy," says the Judge.

Three other versions, from Illinois (2) and Georgia (1) dated by storytellers as having been known in 1876, 1912, and 1920 place the hitchhiker in a horse-drawn vehicle; Professor Jones has also called attention to a Chinese story collected from immigrants in California in which the ghost of a beautiful young girl *walks* with a young man along the road to her parents' home, whereupon she disappears. In an interesting counterpart to the American legend, the Chinese girl walks *behind* the man (just as the hitchhiker almost invariably sits in the car's backseat or rumble seat), so that he must turn around in order to notice her disappearance. Also, the Chinese father's reaction is a clear parallel of the scene in later accounts: "Yes, that is the precise place where she was killed. It was her spirit which led you here." With such earlier non-automotive versions as this in mind, we can easily agree with Louis Jones's conclusion that "The nonghostly motifs have tended to die out and the more vigorous ghostlore has adapted itself to the changes of transportational environment, as the horse gave way to the auto and bus." It might be added, however, that modern automotive vanishing hitchhikers are documented in far greater numbers and places than any earlier stories involving foot- or horse-powered travel, and that not all links between foreign and domestic versions or nineteenth and twentieth-century versions of the story complex have been discovered by any means.

One such apparent missing link was produced in 1954 by

Haruo Aoki of UCLA when he published this tale of a Korean hitchhiking ghost which bears striking similarities to several of the American variants. He heard it in 1941, which suggests that any cross-influence between the United States and the Far East (possibly through Oriental workers in the West) must have been accomplished at least a few years before the outbreak of war with Japan.

J

About midnight a taxi driver of Guntaku Cab Company in Kunsan [Korea] received a telephone call from the municipal crematory asking for a cab. He picked up a young lady of twenty or so in front of the crematory and was told to drive to the hardware store of a Mr. Shimo. [Aoki added, "My grandmother was a very good friend of Mr. and Mrs. Shimo and told me that they recalled the incident."] When the cab arrived at Mr. Shimo's place on Meiji Street the girl told the driver she did not have the fare and asked him to wait until she could go into the house to get it. Because Mr. Shimo had kept a store at the same location for years and was a respected citizen, the driver waited outside without any misgivings. The girl, however, did not reappear. Finally the driver became impatient and knocked at the closed door. After repeated attempts to arouse somebody in the house, sleepy-looking Mrs. Shimo showed up and asked the driver what he wanted. She seemed to know nothing about the girl's ride. However, after the driver had described the young lady, Mrs. Shimo showed him a picture of her daughter on the wall. The daughter had died a few days before and her body had been sent to the same crematory. The driver recognized her immediately and became fatally ill.

The portrait-identification motif, as we have already noted, has become a regular feature of many American versions. Its *source* abroad (rather than merely its occurrence) was strongly suggested by a published account of a legend that had swept

Petersburg (now Leningrad), Russia, in 1890 which was discovered in 1964 by William B. Edgerton in Moscow's Lenin Library. From the December 16, 1890, *The Citizen* (Edgerton's translation):

K

There is a story going about town that is worthy of attention. The only question is whether it is true, and to what extent. The other day, somewhere on Sergievskaya Street, or near it, a priest carrying the holy sacraments came to a certain apartment after mass. A young man answered the door.

"I was asked to come here and give the sacraments to a sick man," said the priest.

"You must have made a mistake. Nobody lives here except me."

"No, a lady came up to me today and gave me this very address and asked me to give the sacraments to the man who lives here."

The young apartment dweller was perplexed.

"Why look, that is the very woman who asked me to come," said the priest, pointing to a woman's portrait hanging on the wall.

"That is the portrait of my dead mother."

Awe, fear, terror seized hold of the young man. Under the impression of all this he took communion.

That evening he lay dead.

Such is the story.

A version of this story—"The Ghost in Search of Help for a Dying Man"—involving a doctor rather than a priest, was reported from London in 1942, and one California "Vanishing Hitchhiker" tale told about 1932 mentions that the ghost, an old woman, is trying to get to the bedside of her dying son. The driver of the car arrives, following his passenger's disappearance, just minutes after the young man has died. (It is assumed that the ghost had made it to the deathbed in time theory of "polygenesis"

to console her son.) Some folklorists might argue, incidentally, that identification by means of a portrait is a "natural" enough detail to have been invented independently more than once. The theory is called "polygenesis," and it is probably unprovable either way.

The quest for the ultimate origin of "The Vanishing Hitchhiker" and its variations pretty well comes to a halt at this point, at least until further nineteenth-century and foreign prototypes are discovered. But updated and localized treatments of the legend continue to flourish in modern folklore, suggesting that the old ghost tale must have some important appeal to contemporary folk. In Hawaii, for example, where forms of the story have been told since the mid-1930s, the hitchhiker has been associated with the ancient Hawaiian volcano goddess Pele. Katharine Luomala of the University of Hawaii and her students collected forty-eight hitchhiking-Pele variants and three more in which Pele is a disappearing guest in a Honolulu luxury hotel. In a totally different urban setting—on Cline Avenue separating Gary, Indiana, from East Chicago and Hammond—folklorist Philip Brandt George of Indiana University discovered "The Vanishing Hitchhiker" combined with stories about the traditional Mexican spirit *La Llorona*, or "The Weeping Woman." Perhaps the most striking adaptation to an American cultural tradition is the merging of "The Vanishing Hitchhiker" with the Mormon "Three Nephite" tradition. As reported by Utah folklorist William A. Wilson, this combination "from 1955 to 1965—was the most popular and influential story in Mormon folklore. . . ."

According to the *Book of Mormon*, the three Nephites were disciples of Christ who were granted earthly existence until His Second Coming, and (quoting the Latter-day Saints' scripture) they ". . . can show themselves unto whatsoever man it seemeth them good" (3 Nephi, 28:30). Oral accounts of their appearances—usually singly, to Mormons in times of need or distress—have circulated among the Mormons since the late nineteenth century, with the first hitchhiking-Nephite story reported in 1938. The popular version of the 1950s and 1960s usually included a specific warning to participate in the Mormon food storage program, a hedge against future economic calamaties urged on members by the Latter-day Saints Church since 1936 and repeatedly stressed by Church authorities. Some of these hitchhiking-Nephite stories are projected back in time to the pioneer period, but most of them are modernized, as illustrated in this example:

L

A Relief Society [Mormon women's group] sister of our ward [Mormon congregation] in Ogden, Utah, said she attended a testimony meeting in another ward of our stake [Mormon grouping of several wards]. A woman bearing her testimony there told this story. She was traveling to attend the Temple sessions with a friend of hers one Saturday morning. As she entered Ogden Canyon, she saw an older man hitchhiking along the side of the road. She normally did not make it a practice to pick up strangers, but he looked tired and he had "a kind face" so she slowed to a stop and inquired if he would like to ride with them. He consented gratefully, and they continued their journey. After they had talked for a few minutes, he asked where the two ladies were going. When they told him they were going to the Temple he began to talk of the Welfare Program. He told them that there would come in the not too distant future a time of great need. He told them to store staple foods and clothes for at least a period of two years. [Official Church policy recommends a one-year food supply, but folklore frequently mentions two years.] He said that none would be exempt from this period of famine and that all should make preparations for the pestilence. The woman who was driving was amazed at his talk and she turned toward him to ask him if he were also a member of the Church. He had disappeared; he was not sitting on the seat beside her as he had been only a minute previous. The ladies both looked back upon the road and to the sides of them, but no one was to be seen. They said the man had been short in stature with blue eyes and grey mustache and beard. He had been dressed in an old black coat with tails, similar to those worn at the time of the organization of the Church in the eighteen hundreds.

Professor Wilson, who compared fifty "Nephite-Vanishing Hitchhiker" legends in the Brigham Young University Folklore Archives, points out that the reference in many versions to the travel of Mormons to a Latter-day Saint temple, where only qualified members may enter, lends credence to the stories among Mormon folk. Also, Wilson feels that some Mormons identified the Korean War and the Cold War with the disasters the *Book of Mormon* prophesied would occur before the final apocalypse for which food was supposed to be stored. Thus this period was conducive to the spread of the legends. Mormon church authorities downplayed the possibility of any of these Nephite stories being authentic messages from God, for, as Wilson puts it, "If He had something important to say to the entire church, God would certainly not bypass His chosen leaders and attempt to spread the message abroad by sending Nephites hitchhiking through the countryside." Apparently this logical reasoning has not bothered the many Mormon folk who find the story to be one acceptable way to help rationalize the great mystery of revelation upon which much of their doctrine is based.

As varieties of modern folklore grew and spread they have had to adapt in order to survive. (A biological metaphor is apt, and folklorists have long spoken of "the life histories of folktales" and regional "oikotypes" [ecotypes].) Thus we have seen that the retellings of "The Vanishing Hitchhiker" in the United States have varied greatly, bringing in current events (such as the World Wars), local persons (e.g. cab drivers), Mormon "Nephites," a Spanish-American weeping-woman spirit, and countless specifics of places, names, photographs, clothing, and the behavior of the wandering ghosts. Nevertheless, the legend always retains the same basic plot and a powerful core of wonder—about the strangers we see along the highways and about the fate of those who died young and tragically. As drivers of automobiles ourselves, we imagine that we might sometime pick up one of these lost souls and experience first-hand the things the legends speak of. A literary ghost story such as Washington Irving's "Legend of Sleepy Hollow" makes a fine schoolbook piece, but being frozen in print and remote in setting it could never keep pace with the ghost and horror lore in oral tradition. Schoolchildren *read* Irving's story (at least when they are required to), but they do not *tell* it. They certainly do tell "The Death Car" and "The Vanishing Hitch-hiker."

Another major development in the long and complex history of the roadside ghost is almost predictable, given the nature of folklore and the changing times. Lydia M. Fish of the State University College of New York at Buffalo discovered in more than sixty texts she and her students collected locally that the current hitchhiker is likely to be "a beautiful young hippie clad in shining white" who engages his host or hosts in a conversation about Jesus and His Second Coming before disappearing. Sometimes he even leaves his seat belt buckled up. Actually, up to the disappearance, and perhaps taking the description "shining white" for poetic license, the story is believable, though we have no firsthand version. Hitchhiking youngsters do sometimes have a cause to promote, and Jesus may be it. Here is an example of "Jesus on the Thruway" told in 1972 by a nineteen-year-old man from Amherst, New York, a suburb of Buffalo:

M

My friend John Hogan who I went to DeSalles High with told me this. He goes to St. John Fisher College now. His fiancee and her aunt who's a nun, were going down the Thruway and they picked this hitchhiker up at the entrance. They were coming from Syracuse and going to Rochester. The guy wanted to know if they had ever heard the gospel and if they knew Jesus. Then he'd go, "He's coming soon" and then next thing they knew he was gone. They stopped at the nearest service area, pulled up to the gas station attendant and rolled down the window to report it. They were pretty shook up and felt kind of dumb. The guy said he wasn't surprised and would they believe that about twenty other people had reported the same story. . . . My father works as a toll collector at the Williamsville Thruway entrance and he heard a lot about it.

One wonders about the nun in this story. She seems to have no function in the plot and may be simply a survival of the prophetic-nun motif in earlier New York State legends.

In a southwest version, the pious passenger is picked up (like many of the female ghosts of the past) on a lonely road at night during a storm. This text was collected by folklorist Keith Cunningham in Arizona in 1978:

N

Someone Miss Packard knew, unfortunately, I cannot remember the person's name, was driving on a deserted road towards Holbrook on a cold, rainy night. As she was driving, she saw a figure on the side of the road, soaking wet trying to thumb a ride. She felt sorry for the person, stopped the car, and a young man sat down in the front seat. After a long period of silence he said, "Jesus is coming again." She turned to look at him, and he was gone.

As if the life history of this legend is not baffling enough, consider that there is a prototypical "Vanishing Hitchhiker" story (*not* the true ancestor of our legend) in the New Testament in which the Apostle Philip baptizes an Ethiopian who picks him up in a chariot, then disappears (see Acts 8:26–39). And also, contemporary with the special adaptations of the legend, such as the Mormon or counterculture variants, there continue to be many new accounts of the old ghost story, including occasional alleged firsthand reports, such as the following, collected in 1969:

O

I was riding from Greenville to Winston-Salem [North Carolina] and decided to take the old road to Greensboro. It was early dawn and the month was October. I was very drowsy but suddenly woke up when I saw a young girl dressed in a long gown standing on the highway. I stopped and asked her if I could help her. She said that her date had gotten mad when she stopped his advances and had made her get out and walk. I offered to take her home, and she accepted. She didn't say much on the way. When we got there, I got out and came around to open the door for her, but she was gone. I couldn't understand it and went up to the house and rang the bell. When an elderly lady answered, I asked for Mary. "Not again," was all she said. I said, "What?" And she explained that Mary had been killed in a car wreck. I was about the fifth person in eight years that had tried to bring her home. It sure shook me up knowing that I had driven a ghost around.

I just hope that poor girl gets wherever it is she's going.

So do I! But let us move on in the next chapter to another popular automotive legend involving an eager teenage boy, his reluctant date, and a different kind of shock when he goes around the car to open her door.

NOTES

"The Death Car"

University of Utah students who have told me versions of "The Death Car" include Marc Ordman, Fall 1969 class (quoted in this chapter), and Laura Fife and Kirsten Jensen, Fall 1971. Richard M. Dorson discussed "The Death Car" in *American Folklore* (University of Chicago Press, 1959), pp. 250–252; his Mecosta, Michigan, text with discussion and annotation appeared both in Dorson's *Negro Folktales in Michigan* (Cambridge, Mass.: Harvard University Press, 1956), p. 99, and *American Negro Folktales* (Greenwich, Conn.: Fawcett Premier Books, 1967), pp. 298–299. Stewart Sanderson's "The Folklore of the Motor-car" was published in *Folklore* [journal of the English Folklore Society], 80 (1969), pp. 241–252, with "The Ineradicable Blood-Stain" summarized on page 250. The Maryland "Death Car" text is from George Carey's *Maryland Folk Legends and Folk Songs* (Cambridge, Maryland: Tidewater Publishers, 1971), p. 73.

"The Philanderer's Porsche"

Ann Landers' column contained "The Philanderer's Porsche" version quoted here on November 4, 1979. Stewart Sanderson discussed the "Sale of Car for the Husband's Mistress" in "The Folklore of the Motor-car" (p. 249). He listed the following three occurrences, all specifying amounts of money and models of cars—1948 or 1949 in Edinburgh, 1962 in Leeds, and 1969 printed in *The Autocar*. In a footnote Sanderson cited evidence suggesting that the story might be based on an actual event publicized in English newspapers in 1948: "If, on checking, this proves to be so, this will probably be the first of these folktales to have its *point-de-départ* traced." To my knowledge no one has yet located this alleged source.

"The Vanishing Hitchhiker"

"The Vanishing Hitchhiker" is the only urban legend with a specific motif number assigned to it in the standard folkloristic reference works. See motif E332.3.3.1. in Ernest W. Baughman, *Type and Motif Index of the Folktales of England and North America,* Indiana University Folklore Series, No. 20 (The Hague: Mouton and Co., 1966) for a summary of this and related themes as well as bibliographic references.

Published versions of "The Vanishing Hitchhiker" are listed below in chronological order with commentary and identification of the sources of texts quoted in this chapter in square brackets:

Jon Lee, *The Golden Mountain: Chinese Tales Told in California,* Asian Folklore Society and Social Life Monographs, vol.

13 (Taiwan, China: The Orient Cultural Service, 1972). Originally published as Occasional Papers, Manuscript Series, No. 1 (San Francisco: WPA, 1940). [No. 9, "The Daughter Returns," pp. 7–8, is discussed in this chapter.]

Grace Partridge Smith, "Folklore from Egypt [a region in southern Illinois]," *Journal of American Folklore*, 54 (1941), 48–59. ["The Traveling Spirit," pp. 54–55; ghost enters a bus but vanishes when it crosses a bridge. Identified as a person who died at the spot where picked up.]

South Carolina Folk Tales, Compiled by Workers of the Writers' Program of the WPA (Columbia: University of South Carolina, 1941). ["The Girl in the Swamp," pp. 72–74. Example B in this chapter is in footnote no. 187 on p. 72.]

Rosalie Hankey, "California Ghosts," *California Folklore Quarterly*, 1 (1942), 155–177. [Thirteen texts of "Stories of the Hitchhiking Dead." The version from Berkeley which Hankey checked against police records is on p. 173, and the ghost of a woman traveling to the bedside of her dying son is on p. 175.]

Richard K. Beardsley and Rosalie Hankey, "The Vanishing Hitchhiker," *California Folklore Quarterly*, 1 (1942), 303–335. [A comparative study of seventy-nine versions. Example C is no. 8, p. 320; Example D is no. 14, pp. 324–325; E is no. 18, p. 327; and F is no. 11, p. 322.]

Richard K. Beardsley and Rosalie Hankey, "A History of the Vanishing Hitchhiker," *California Folklore Quarterly*, 2 (1943), 13–25. [An attempt to sort out the development of materials summarized in the item preceding. Example G in this chapter is quoted on p. 20, and the London example of "The Ghost in Search of Help for a Dying Man" is in footnote no. 19, p. 17.]

William Hugh Jansen, "Folklore Items from a Teacher's Notebook," *Hoosier Folklore Bulletin*, 2 (1943), 1–8. [Three texts of "The Vanishing Hitchhiker," pp. 2–4; in two she wears a white formal dress under a black cape.]

Anne Clark, "The Ghost of White Rock," *Backwoods to Border: Publications of the Texas Folklore Society*, No. 18 (1943), 143–147. [Ghost in a sheer white dress, dripping wet, rides in rumble seat; she had drowned three weeks earlier in White Rock Lake. Another version of this story is given in Joe Nick Patoski's article "GGGhost Stories," *Texas Monthly*, October, 1978, p. 136.]

Louis C. Jones, "Hitchhiking Ghosts in New York," *Califor-*

The Classic Automobile Legends

nia Folklore Quarterly, 3 (1944), 284–292. [Modified some of Beardsley and Hankey's conclusions, and reported on forty-nine New York versions. Example H in this chapter is on p. 289.]

William Marion Miller, "Another Phantom Hitchhiker Story," *Hoosier Folklore,* 5 (1946), 40–41. [Occurrence near Canton, Ohio.]

William Marion Miller, "Another Vanishing Hitchhiker Story," *Hoosier Folklore,* 6 (1947), 76. [From Brown County, Ind.]

Ernest W. Baughman, "The Hitchhiking Ghost," *Hoosier Folklore,* 6 (1947), 77–78. [Version dated to 1876 from Watseka, Ill., a horse-drawn carriage.]

Edmund Burke, "Funnel Country," *New York Folklore Quarterly,* 4 (1948), 256–267. [Version set on the Waverly-Owego Road, near Elmira, a place called "Devil's Elbow."]

Hector Lee, *The Three Nephites: The Substance and Significance of the Legend in Folklore,* University of New Mexico Publications in Language and Literature, No. 2 (Albuquerque: University of New Mexico Press, 1949). [No. 57a. "The Hitchhiking 'Ghost' Nephite," pp. 147–148, an example collected in 1946 in Green River, Utah. Hitchhiker predicts end of war and that the car will carry a corpse later in the day; thirdhand report of a personal experience.]

Gerard T. Hurley, "The Vanishing Hitchhiker Again," *Western Folklore,* 11 (1952), 46. [Set in the Catskills, New York, about 1933; little old lady hitchhiking to her son's house.]

Vance Randolph, "Folktales from Arkansas," *Journal of American Folklore,* 65 (1952), 159–166. ["A Pretty Girl in the Road," pp. 163–164 is Example I in this chapter. Reprinted in Randolph's *The Devil's Pretty Daughter and Other Ozark Folktales* (New York: Columbia University Press, 1955, pp. 79–81.)]

Margo Skinner, "The Vanishing Hitchhiker Again," *Western Folklore,* 12 (1953), 136–137. [Report of a well known ghost on the road between La Porte and Michigan City, Indiana, several times reported in the press.]

Mildred R. Larson, "The Vanishing Hitchhiker Again," *New York Folklore Quarterly,* 9 (1953), 51–52. [Several versions discussed, example quoted from Kenmore, New York.]

"Vanishing Hitchhiker," *Western Folklore,* 13 (1954), 54. [Report in Los Angeles *Daily News,* June 10, 1953, of "the ghost of a *norteamericano* hitchhiker" in Mexico.]

43

THE VANISHING HITCHHIKER

Haruo Aoki, "A Hitchhiking Ghost in Korea," *Western Folklore*, 13 (1954), 280–281. [Source of Example J in this chapter.]

Leonard W. Roberts, *South from Hell-fer-Sartin: Kentucky Mountain Folk Tales* (Lexington, Ky.: University of Kentucky Press, 1955). [Text no. 98a, p. 190, "Spirit of the Wreck," is set "up in New York".]

Louis C. Jones, *Things that Go Bump in the Night* (New York: Hill and Wang, 1959). [Chapter six, "The Ghostly Hitchhiker," used the materials of Jones's 1944 article but reported a total of seventy-five versions from author's New York collection. Called the ghost "Hitchhiking Hattie."]

Jan Harold Brunvand, "An Indiana Storyteller Revisited," *Midwest Folklore*, 11 (1961), 5–14. [Collected in 1959 from a storyteller from whom it was also collected in 1942; text is on pp. 10–11. She sits in the backseat because she has a cold.]

William B. Edgerton, "The Ghost in Search of Help for a Dying Man," *Journal of the Folklore Institute*, 5 (1968), 31–41. [Example K in this chapter is on p. 32.]

Stewart Sanderson, "The Folklore of the Motor-car," *Folklore* [London], 80 (1969), 241–252. [Summarized British version on p. 251.]

George G. Carey, *Maryland Folk Legends and Folk Songs* (Cambridge, Maryland: Tidewater Publishers, 1971). ["Ghostly Hitchhiker" from a Salisbury, Maryland, man who came from West Virginia, pp. 81–82.]

Douglas J. McMillan, "The Vanishing Hitchhiker in Eastern North Carolina," *North Carolina Folklore*, 20 (1972), 123–128. [Eleven versions reported, five printed, of which Example O in this chapter is on pp. 124–125.]

Katharine Luomala, "Disintegration and Regeneration, The Hawaiian Phantom Hitchhiker Legend," *Fabula: Zeitschrift für Erzählforschung*, 13 (1972), 20–59.

Philip Brandt George, "The Ghost of Cline Avenue," *Indiana Folklore*, 5 (1972), 56–91.

William A. Wilson, "The Vanishing Hitchhiker Among the Mormons," *Indiana Folklore*, 8 (1975), 80–97. [Example L in this chapter is on pp. 84–85.]

William Lynwood Montell, *Ghosts Along the Cumberland: Deathlore in the Kentucky Foothills* (Knoxville: University of Tennessee Press, 1975). [Twenty texts, nos. 317 through 336, are grouped under the heading "The Vanishing Hitchhiker" on pages 118 to 129, but these really constitute a number of similar tales which are not necessarily related. Of particular interest are five legends (collected from 1961 to 1965) telling of a non-hitchhiking ghost riding horseback behind a person (nos. 318 through 322) and four texts of "The Vanishing Hitchhiker" proper (nos. 333 through 336) collected in 1968 and 1969 and invariably including the motif of the borrowed jacket or coat. The ghostly rider is identifed either by a description or by her name.]

Susan Smith, "Urban Tales," in Edith Fowke, ed., *Folklore of Canada* (Toronto: McClelland and Stewart, 1976), pp. 262–268. [Example A in this chapter, "The Disappearing Hitchhiker," p. 265.]

Lydia M. Fish, "Jesus on the Thruway: The Vanishing Hitchhiker Strikes Again," *Indiana Folklore*, 9 (1976), 5–13. [Example M in this chapter is on pp. 9–10.]

Ruth Ann Musick, *Coffin Hollow and Other Ghost Tales* (Lexington: University of Kentucky Press, 1977). [Eleven West Virginia texts, collected from 1963 to 1968, contained "The Vanishing Hitchhiker" motif. The dates of occurrence, when specified, were said to be from the "early 1900s" through the 1930s, and some, by implication, were recent. Considerable variation in details and style is perhaps partly explained by the fact that most informants wrote out their texts. Tales involved are nos. 20, 71–77, 79, 80, and 83.]

Editor [Keith Cunningham], "The Vanishing Hitchhiker in Arizona—Almost," *Southwest Folklore*, 3 (1979), 46–50. [Example N in this chapter is on p. 46; also contained four texts of versions which differed significantly from the subtypes established by earlier folklore scholars' writings.]

Lydia Fish (see above, 1976) also provided some information on an MA thesis at the State University College of New York, Oneonta, Cooperstown Graduate Program, 1966, by Jansen L. Cox, titled "The Vanishing Hitchhiker." Of forty-nine texts with male hitchhikers, she reported (p. 7) that Cox has twelve Nephites, an angel, one rider identified as St. Joseph and one as Jesus.

Carl Carmer's story "The Lavender Evening Dress" from *Dark Trees to the Wind* (1949) is based on "The Vanishing Hitchhiker." It is reprinted in John T. Flanagan and Arthur Palmer Hudson, ed., *Folklore in American Literature* (Evanston, Ill.: Row, Peterson, 1958), pp. 99–101. For a "Vanishing Hitchhiker" reference in Jesse Stuart's fiction see *Kentucky Folklore Record*, 9 (1963), 43.

"The Vanishing Hitchhiker" has been the inspiration for several songs and television plots. Perhaps the best known of these popular-culture adaptations is Dickey Lee's recording on a 45 rpm single (TCF-102) of the song "Laurie," which is subtitled in parentheses "Strange Things Happen." Laurie, an "angel of a girl," meets the narrator at a dance, walks home with him, and borrows his sweater; later she is revealed to have "died a year ago today," and the sweater is found "lyin' there upon her grave."

In Leon Festinger, Henry W. Riecken, and Stanley Schachter's study *When Prophecy Fails* (Minneapolis: University of Minnesota Press, 1956), a version of "The Vanishing Hitchhiker" is told as part of a sociological study of traditional religious practices; see pp. 239–240.

3 | "The Hook" and Other Teenage Horrors

Growing Up Scared

People of all ages love a good scare. Early childlore is full of semi-serious spooky stories and ghastly threats, while the more sophisticated black humor of Little Willies, Bloody Marys, Dead Babies, and other cycles of sick jokes enters a bit later. Among the favorite readings at school are Edgar Allan Poe's blood-soaked tales, and favorite stories at summer camp tell of maniacal ax-murderers and deformed giants lurking in the dark forest to ambush unwary Scouts. Halloween spook houses and Hollywood horror films cater to the same wish to push the level of tolerable fright as far as possible.

The ingredients of horror fiction change little through time, but the style of such stories does develop, even in oral tradition. In their early teens young Americans apparently reject the overdramatic and unbelievable juvenile "scaries" and adopt a new lore of more plausible tales with realistic settings. That is, they begin to enjoy urban legends, especially those dealing with "folks" like themselves—dating couples, students, and baby-sitters—who are subjected to grueling ordeals and horrible threats. (We looked at one example, "The Boyfriend's Death," in Chapter 1.)

One consistent theme in these teenage horrors is that as the adolescent moves out from home into the larger world, the world's dangers may close in on him or her. Therefore, although the immediate purpose of many of these legends is to produce a good scare, they also serve to deliver a warning: Watch out! This could happen to you! Furthermore, the horror tales often contain thinly-disguised sexual themes which are, perhaps, implicit in the nature of such plot situations as parking in a lovers' lane or baby-sitting (playing house) in a strange home. These sexual elements furnish both a measure of further entertainment and definite cautionary notices about the world's actual dangers. Thus, from the teenagers' own major fears, concerns, and experiences, spring their favorite "true" oral stories.

sexual themes

The chief current example of this genre of urban legend—one that is even older, more popular, and more widespread than "The Boyfriend's Death"—is the one usually called "The Hook."

"The Hook"

On Tuesday, November 8, 1960, the day when Americans went to the polls to elect John F. Kennedy as their thirty-fifth president, thousands of people must have read the following letter from a teenager in the popular newspaper column written by Abigail Van Buren:

> DEAR ABBY: If you are interested in teenagers, you will print this story. I don't know whether it's true or not, but it doesn't matter because it served its purpose for me:
> A fellow and his date pulled into their favorite "lovers' lane" to listen to the radio and do a little necking. The music was interrupted by an announcer who said there was an escaped convict in the area who had served time for rape and robbery. He was described as having a hook instead of a right hand. The couple became frightened and drove away. When the boy took his girl home, he went around to open the car door for her. Then he saw—a

hook on the door handle! I don't think I will ever park to make out as long as I live. I hope this does the same for other kids.

JEANETTE

This juicy story seems to have emerged in the late 1950s, sharing some common themes with "The Death Car'" and "The Vanishing Hitchhiker" and then, as shown in Chapter 1, influencing "The Boyfriend's Death" as that legend developed in the early 1960s. The story of "The Hook" (or "The Hookman") really needed no national press report to give it life or credibility, because the teenage oral-tradition underground had done the job well enough long before the election day of 1960. Teenagers all over the country knew about "The Hook" by 1959, and like other modern legends the basic plot was elaborated with details and became highly localized.

One of my own students, originally from Kansas, provided this specific account of where the event supposedly occurred:

> Outside of "Mac" [McPherson, Kansas], about seven miles out towards Lindsborg, north on old highway 81 is an old road called "Hookman's Road." It's a curved road, a traditional parking spot for the kids. When I was growing up it [the legend] was popular, and that was back in the '60's, and it was old then.

Another student told a version of the story that she had heard from her baby-sitter in Albuquerque in 1960:

> . . . over the radio came an announcement that a crazed killer with a hook in place of a hand had escaped from the local insane asylum. The girl got scared and begged the boy to take her home. He got mad and stepped on the gas and roared off. When they got to her house, he got out and went around to the other side of the car to let her out. There on the door handle was a bloody hook.

But these two students were told, after arriving in Salt Lake City, that it had actually occurred *here* in Memory Grove, a well-wooded city park. "Oh, no," a local student in the class insisted, "This couple was parked outside of Salt Lake City *in a mountain canyon* one night, and . . ." It turned out that virtually every student in the class knew the story as adapted in some way to their hometowns.

Other folklorists have reported collecting "The Hook" in Maryland, Wisconsin, Indiana, Illinois, Kansas, Texas, Arkansas, Oregon, and Canada. Some of the informants' comments echo Dear Abby's correspondent in testifying to the story's effect (to discourage parking) even when its truth was suspect. The students said, "I believe that it *could* happen, and this makes it seem real," or "I don't really [believe it], but it's pretty scary; I sort of hope it didn't happen."

Part of the great appeal of "The Hook"—one of the most popular adolescent scare stories—must lie in the tidiness of the plot. Everything fits. On the other hand, the lack of loose ends would seem to be excellent testimony to the story's near impossibility. After all, what are the odds that a convicted criminal or crazed maniac would be fitted with a hook for a missing hand, that this same threatening figure would show up precisely when a radio warning had been broadcast of his escape, and that the couple would drive away rapidly just at the instant the hookman put his hook through the door handle? Besides, why wouldn't he try to open the door with his good hand, and how is it that the boy—furious at the interruption of their lovemaking—is still willing to go around politely to open the girl's door when they get home? Too much, too much—but it makes a great story.

In an adolescent novel titled *Dinky Hocker Shoots Smack!*, M. E. Kerr captured the way teenagers often react to such legends—with cool acceptance that it might have happened, and that's good enough:

> She told Tucker this long story about a one-armed man who was hanging around a lovers' lane in Prospect Park [Brooklyn]. There were rumors that he tried to get in the cars and carry off the girls. He banged on the windshields with his hooked wooden arm and frothed at the mouth.

He only said two words: *bloody murder;* and his voice was high and hoarse.

Dinky claimed this girl who went to St. Marie's was up in Prospect Park one night with a boyfriend. The girl and her boyfriend began discussing the one-armed man while they were parked. They both got frightened and decided to leave. The boy dropped the girl off at her house, and drove home. When he got out of his car, he found this hook attached to his door handle.

Dinky said, "They must have driven off just as he was about to open the door."

"I thought you weren't interested in the bizarre, anymore," Tucker said.

"It's a true story."

"It's still bizarre."

A key detail lacking in the *Dinky Hocker* version, however, is the boyfriend's frustrated anger resulting in their leaving the scene in a great hurry. Almost invariably the boy guns the motor and roars away: ". . . so he revs up the car and he goes torquing out of there." Or, "The boy floored the gas pedal and zoomed away," or "Her boyfriend was annoyed and the car screeched off. . . ." While this behavior is essential to explain the sudden sharp force that tears loose the maniac's hook, it is also a reminder of the original sexual purpose of the parking, at least on the boy's part. While Linda Dégh saw "the natural dread of the handicapped," and "the boy's disappointment and suddenly recognized fear as an adequate explanation for the jump start of the car," folklorist Alan Dundes disagreed, mainly because of the curtailed sex quest in the plot.

Dundes, taking a Freudian line, interpreted the hook itself as a phallic symbol which penetrates the girl's door handle (or bumps seductively against her window) but which is torn off (symbolic of castration) when the car starts abruptly. Girls who tell the story, Dundes suggests, "are not afraid of what a man lacks, but of what he has"; a date who is "all hands" may really want to "get his hooks into her." Only the girl's winding up the window or insisting upon going home at once saves her, and the date has to "pull out fast" before he begins to act like a sex maniac himself. The radio—turned on originally for soft, romantic background music—introduces instead "the consciencelike voice from society," a warning that the girl heeds and the boy usually scorns. Dundes concluded that this popular legend "reflects a very real dating practice, one which produces anxiety . . . particularly for girls."

"The Killer in the Backseat"

A similar urban legend also involves cars and an unseen potential assailant; this time a man threatens a woman who is driving alone at night. The following version of "The Killer in the Backseat" was contributed in 1967 by a University of Utah student who had heard other versions set in Denver and Aurora, Colorado:

> A woman living in the city [i.e., Salt Lake City] was visiting some friends in Ogden. When she got into her car in front of this friend's house, she noticed that a car started up right behind her car. It was about 2:00 in the morning, and there weren't any other cars on the road. After she had driven to the highway, she began to think that this car was following her. Some of the time he would drive up real close to her car, but he wouldn't ever pass. She was really scared to death and kept speeding to try to get away from him.
>
> When she got to Salt Lake, she started running stop lights to get away from him, but he would run right through them too. So when she got to her driveway she pulled in really fast, and this guy pulled in right behind her. She just laid on the horn, and her husband came running out. Just then, the guy jumped out of the car, and her husband ran over and said, "What the hell's goin' on here?" So he grabbed the guy, and his wife said, "This man's followed me all the way from Ogden." The man said, "I followed your wife because I was going to work,

and as I got into my car, I noticed when I turned my lights on, a man's head bob down in her back seat." So the husband went over to her backseat, opened the door, and pulled this guy from out of the backseat.

This legend first appeared in print in 1968 in another version, also—coincidentally—set in Ogden, Utah, but collected at Indiana University, Bloomington. (This shows how the presence of folklorists in a locality will influence the apparent distribution patterns of folk material.) Twenty further texts have surfaced at Indiana University with, as usual, plenty of variations and localizations. In many instances the pursuing driver keeps flashing his headlights between the high and low beam in order to restrain the assailant who is popping up and threatening to attack the driver. Sometimes the pursuer is a burly truck driver or other tough-looking character, and in several of the stories the supposed would-be attacker (the pursuing rescuer) is specifically said to be a black man. (Both motifs clearly show white middle class fears of minorities or of groups believed to be socially inferior.)

In a more imaginative set of these legends the person who spots the dangerous man in back is a gas station attendant who pretends that a ten dollar bill offered by the woman driver in payment for gas is counterfeit. With this ruse he gets her safely away from her car before calling the police. In another version of the story, a passing motorist sharply warns the woman driver to roll up her window and follow him, driving in exactly the same manner he does. She obeys, speeding and weaving along the highway, until a suspected assailant—usually carrying an ax—is thrown from his perch on the roof of her car.

"The Baby-sitter and the Man Upstairs"

Just as a lone woman may unwittingly be endangered by a hidden man while she is driving at night, a younger one may face the same hazard in a strange home. The horror legend of "The Baby-sitter and the Man Upstairs," similar in structure to

"The Killer in the Backseat," is possibly a later variation of the same story relocated to fit teenagers' other direct experiences. This standard version is from a fourteen-year-old Canadian boy (1973):

> There was this baby-sitter that was in Montreal baby-sitting for three children in a big house. She was watching TV when suddenly the phone rang. The children were all in bed. She picked up the phone and heard this guy on the other end laughing hysterically. She asked him what it was that he wanted, but he wouldn't answer and then hung up. She worried about it for a while, but then thought nothing more of it and went back to watching the movie.
>
> Everything was fine until about fifteen minutes later when the phone rang again. She picked it up and heard the same voice laughing hysterically at her, and then hung up. At this point she became really worried and phoned the operator to tell her what had been happening. The operator told her to calm down and that if he called again to try and keep him on the line as long as possible and she would try to trace the call.
>
> Again about fifteen minutes later the guy called back and laughed hysterically at her. She asked him why he was doing this, but he just kept laughing at her. He hung up and about five seconds later the operator called. She told the girl to get out of the house at once because the person who was calling was calling from the upstairs extension. She slammed down the phone and just as she was turning to leave she saw the man coming down the stairs laughing hysterically with a bloody butcher knife in his hand and meaning to kill her. She ran out onto the street but he didn't follow. She called the police and they came and caught the man, and discovered that he had murdered all the children.

The storyteller added that he had heard the story from a friend whose brother's girlfriend was the baby-sitter involved.

By now it should come as no surprise to learn that the same

story had been collected two years earlier (1971) some 1500 miles southwest of Montreal, in Austin, Texas, and also in Bloomington, Indiana, in 1973 in a college dormitory. These three published versions are only samples from the wide distribution of the story in folk tradition. Their similarities and differences provide another classic case of folklore's variation within traditional boundaries. In all three legend texts the hour is late and the baby-sitter is watching television. Two of the callers make threatening statements, while one merely laughs. In all versions the man calls three times at regular intervals before the girl calls the operator, then once more afterwards. In both American texts the operator herself calls the police, and in the Indiana story she commands "Get out of the house immediately; don't go upstairs; don't do anything; just leave the house. When you get out there, there will be policemen outside and they'll take care of it." (One is reminded of the rescuers' orders not to look back at the car in "The Boyfriend's Death.") The Texas telephone operator in common with the Canadian one gives the situation away by adding, "The phone call traces to the upstairs." The murder of the child or children (one, two, or three of them—no pattern) is specified in the American versions: in Texas they are "chopped into little bitty pieces"; in Indiana, "torn to bits." All of the storytellers played up the spookiness of the situation—details that would be familiar to anyone who has ever baby-sat—a strange house, a television show, an unexpected phone call, frightening sounds or threats, the abrupt orders from the operator, and finally the shocking realization at the end that (as in "The Killer in the Backseat") the caller had been there in the house (or behind her) all the time. The technical problems of calling another telephone from an extension of the same number, or the actual procedures of call-tracing, do not seem to worry the storytellers.

Folklorist Sue Samuelson, who examined hundreds of unpublished "Man Upstairs" stories filed in American folklore archives, concluded that the telephone is the most important and emotionally-loaded item in the plot: the assailant is harassing his victim through the device that is her own favorite means of communication. Baby-sitting, Samuelson points out, is an important socializing experience for young women, allowing them to practice their future roles, imposed on them in a male-dominated society, as homemakers and mothers. Significantly, the threatening male figure is *upstairs*—on top of and in control of the girl—as men have traditionally been in the sexual relationship. In killing the children who were in her care, the man brings on the most catastrophic failure any mother can suffer. Another contributing factor in the story is that the baby-sitter herself is too intent on watching television to realize that the children are being murdered upstairs. Thus, the tale is not just another scary story, but conveys a stern admonition to young women to adhere to society's traditional values.

Occasionally these firmly-believed horror legends are transformed from ghastly mysteries to almost comical adventures. The following Arizona version of "The Baby-sitter and the Man Upstairs," collected in 1976, is a good example:

It was August 8, 1969. She was going to baby-sit at the Smiths who had two children, ages five and seven. She had just put the children to bed and went back to the living room to watch TV.

The phone began to ring; she went to answer it; the man on the other end said, "I'm upstairs with the children; you'd better come up."

She hung the phone up immediately, scared to death. She decided that it must be a prank phone call; again she went to watch TV. The phone rang again; she went to answer it, this time more scared than last.

The man said, "I'm upstairs with the children," and described them in detail. So she hung up the phone, not knowing what to do. Should I call the police? Instead she decided, "I'll call the operator. They can trace these phone calls." She called the operator, and the operator said that she would try and do what she could. Approximately ten minutes later the phone rang again; this time she was shaking.

She answered the phone and the man again said, "I'm upstairs with the children; you'd better come quick!" She tried to stay on the phone as long as she could so that the operator could trace the call; this time the man hung up.

She called back, and the operator said, "Run out of the house; the man is on the extension."

She didn't quite know what to do; should she go and get the children? "No," she said, "he's up there; if I go and get the children, I'll be killed too!!"

She ran next door to the neighbor's house and called the police. The sirens came—there must have been at least ten police cars. They went inside the house, ran upstairs, and found not a man, but a seven-year-old child who was sitting next to the phone with a tape recorder. Later they found that a boy down the street had told this young boy to do this next time he had a baby-sitter. You see the boy didn't like his parents going out, and he didn't like having baby-sitters. So he felt this was the only way he could get rid of them. The boys [sic] don't have baby-sitters anymore; now they go to the nursery school.

"The Roommate's Death"

Another especially popular example of the American adolescent shocker story is the widely-known legend of "The Roommate's Death." It shares several themes with other urban legends. As in "The Killer in the Backseat" and "The Babysitter and the Man Upstairs," it is usually a lone woman in the story who is threatened—or thinks she is—by a strange man. As in "The Hook" and "The Boyfriend's Death," the assailant is often said to be an escaped criminal or a maniac. Finally, as in the latter legend, the actual commission of the crime is never described; only the resulting mutilated corpse is. The scratching sounds outside the girl's place of refuge are an additional element of suspense. Here is a version told by a Uni-

versity of Kansas student in 1965 set in Corbin Hall a freshman women's dormitory there:

> These two girls in Corbin had stayed late over Christmas
> vacation. One of them had to wait for a later train, and
> the other wanted to go to a fraternity party given that
> night of vacation. The dorm assistant was in her room—
> sacked out. They waited and waited for the intercom, and
> then they heard this knocking and knocking outside in
> front of the dorm. So the girl thought it was her date and
> she went down. But she didn't come back and she didn't
> come back. So real late that night this other girl heard a
> scratching and gasping down the hall. She couldn't lock
> the door, so she locked herself in the closet. In the morning
> she let herself out and her roommate had had her throat
> cut, and if the other girl had opened the door earlier, she
> [the dead roommate] would have been saved.

At all the campuses where the story is told the reasons for the
girls' remaining alone in the dorm vary, but they are always
realistic and plausible. The girls' homes may be too far away for
them to visit during vacation, such as in Hawaii or a foreign
country. In some cases they wanted to avoid a campus meeting
or other obligation. What separates the two roommates may be
either that one goes out for food, or to answer the door, or to
use the rest room. The girl who is left behind may hear the
scratching noise either at her room door or at the closet door,
if she hides there. Sometimes her hair turns white or grey overnight from the shock of the experience (an old folk motif).
The implication in the story is that some maniac is after her
(as is suspected about the pursuer in "The Killer in the Backseat"); but the truth is that her own roommate needs help,
and she might have supplied it had she only acted more de-
cisively when the noises were first heard. Usually some special
emphasis is put on the victim's fingernails, scratched to bloody
stumps by her desperate efforts to signal for help.

A story told by a California teenager, remembered from

about 1964, seems to combine motifs of "The Baby-sitter and the Man Upstairs" with "The Roommate's Death." The text is unusually detailed with names and the circumstances of the crime:

Linda accepted a baby-sitting job for a wealthy family who lived in a two-storey home up in the hills for whom she had never baby-sat for before. Linda was rather hesitant as the house was rather isolated and so she asked a girlfriend, Sharon, to go along with her, promising Sharon half of the baby-sitting fee she would earn. Sharon accepted Linda's offer and the two girls went up to the big two-storey house.

The night was an especially dark and windy one and rain was threatening. All went well for the girls as they read stories aloud to the three little boys they were sitting for and they had no problem putting the boys to bed in the upstairs part of the house. When this was done, the girls settled down to watching television.

It was not long before the telephone rang. Linda answered the telephone, only to hear the heavy breathing of the caller on the other end. She attempted to elicit a response from the caller but he merely hung up. Thinking little of it and not wanting to panic Sharon, Linda went back to watching her television program, remarking that the caller had dialed a wrong number. Upon receiving the second call at which time the caller first engaged in a bit of heavy breathing and then instructed them to check on the children, the two girls became frightened and decided to call the operator for assistance. The operator instructed the girls to keep the caller on the line as long as possible should he call again so that she might be able to trace the call. The operator would check back with them.

The two girls then decided between themselves that one should stay downstairs to answer the phone. It was Sharon who volunteered to go upstairs. Shortly, the telephone rang again and Linda did as the operator had instructed

59

her. Within a few minutes, the operator called back telling Linda to leave the house immediately with her friend because she had traced the calls to the upstairs phone.

Linda immediately hung up the telephone and proceeded to run to the stairway to call Sharon. She then heard a thumping sound coming from the stairway and when she approached the stairs she saw her friend dragging herself down the stairs by her chin, all of her limbs severed from her body. The three boys also lay dead upstairs in their beds.

Once again, the Indiana University Folklore Archive has provided the best published report on variants of "The Roommate's Death," Linda Dégh's summary of thirty-one texts and several subtypes and related plots collected since 1961. The most significant feature, according to her report, is the frequent appearance of a male rescuer at the end of the story. In one version, for example, two girls are left behind alone in the dorm by their roommate when she goes downstairs for food; they hear noises, and so stay in their room all night without opening the door. Finally the mailman comes around the next morning, and they call him from the window:

> The mailman came in the front door and went up the stairs, and told the girls to stay in their room, that everything was all right but that they were to stay in their rooms [sic]. But the girls didn't listen to him 'cause he had said it was all right, so they came out into the hall. When they opened the door, they saw their girlfriend on the floor with a hatchet in her head.

In other Indiana texts the helpful male is a handyman, a milkman, or the brother of one of the roommates.

According to folklorist Beverly Crane, the male-female characters are only one pair of a series of significant opposites, which also includes home and away, intellectual versus emotional behavior, life and death, and several others. A male is needed to resolve the female's uncertainty—motivated by her emotional fear—about how to act in a new situation. Another male has mutilated and killed her roommate with a blow to her head, "the one part of the body with which women are not supposed to compete." The girls, Crane suggested, are doubly out of place in the beginning, having left the haven of home to engage in intellectual pursuits, and having remained alone in the campus dormitory instead of rejoining the family on a holiday. Ironically, the injured girl must use her fingernails, intended to be long, lovely, feminine adornments, in order to scratch for help. But because her roommate fails to investigate the sound, the victim dies, her once pretty nails now bloody stumps. Crane concluded this ingenious interpretation with these generalizations:

> The points of value implicit in this narrative are then twofold. If women wish to depend on traditional attitudes and responses they had best stay in a place where these attitudes and responses are best able to protect them. If, however, women do choose to venture into the realm of equality with men, they must become less dependent, more self-sufficient, more confident in their own abilities, and, above all, more willing to assume responsibility for themselves and others.

One might not expect to find women's liberation messages embedded in the spooky stories told by teenagers, but Beverly Crane's case is plausible and well argued. Furthermore, it is not at all unusual to find up-to-date social commentary in other modern folklore—witness the many religious and sexual jokes and legends circulated by people who would not openly criticize a church or the traditional social mores. Folklore does not just purvey the old codes of morality and behavior; it can also absorb newer ideas. What needs to be done to analyze this is to collect what Alan Dundes calls "oral-literary criticism," the informants' own comments about their lore. How clearly would the girls who tell these stories perceive—or even accept—the messages extrapolated by scholars? And a related question:

Have any stories with clear liberationist themes replaced older ones cautioning young women to stay home, be good, and— next best—be careful, and call a man if they need help?

"The Pet (or Baby) in the Oven"

The ghastliest believed horror story popular among adolescents (though it is told by older people too) is probably the one involving a living creature put into an oven. An old legend (approximately twenty years), and one that incorporates much older themes, it has recently merged in oral tradition with the baby-sitter stories.

"HOT DOG!"

Folklorists as much as any scholars love to report a new discovery, so it was with understandable pride and delight that Professor Keith Cunningham of Northern Arizona University, Flagstaff, headlined an article in the Winter, 1979, issue of his quarterly journal *Southwest Folklore* "Hot Dog! Another Urban Belief Tale." He provided a sample of this "new" story (one of "more texts . . . than I can count" from the Arizona Friends of Folklore Archive):

> It seems there was an old lady who had been given a microwave oven by her children. After bathing her dog she put it in the microwave to dry it off. Naturally, when she opened the door the dog was cooked from the inside out.

Other Arizona versions, Cunningham revealed, "involve not only dogs, but also birds, cats, and one unfortunate turtle." The tales, he said, illustrate that "modern technology has a way of getting out of control and wreaking ill instead of good."

The legend of the cooked dog or cat has enjoyed a good deal of recent circulation, but it is not a *new* tradition, having been around for twenty years or so in the form of a cautionary tale about the fates of unlucky pets that crawl into untended gas ovens or clothes dryers and are not noticed the next time the appliance is used. Around 1976 I began to hear the microwave-oven variants, and I inserted the following summary example from Utah into the second edition (1978) of my textbook *The Study of American Folklore:* "[a] child . . . accidentally sprinkles the cat with a hose and puts it into a microwave oven to dry out, whereupon the cat explodes (p. 111)." The phrase in the Arizona text, of the animal being "cooked from the inside out," more accurately describes the molecule-jiggling effect of microwaves than the account of the pet exploding in my text (the only way I have heard it). I am told, however, that eyes might possibly pop when bombarded with microwaves, just as eggs or potatoes are said to do if inserted into an oven whole. People's notions about what would happen to a living creature caught in a microwave oven are doubtless colored by a vague fear of the new devices and intensified by such things as the warning signs posted on public-access microwave ovens and the news stories about microwaves beamed by the Soviets into our foreign embassy. Whatever those mysterious invisible waves may do to a person—or to a pacemaker, as the posted warnings imply—they certainly would not be healthy for the family pet. The animal would surely cook and die in the oven, so the fear is quite realistic.

In Spring, 1978, Nancy Schlehuber, a student in my folklore class, read about the story in the textbook, then heard a similar version while at home visiting in Wills Point, Texas. Back in Utah again, she decided to survey the available material for her term project. Ms. Schlehuber collected a few examples of "scientific" versions of the story in which technicians who ought to have known better bypassed built-in safety features and operated their laboratory microwave ovens with open doors, thereby cooking their own insides as they stood nearby. The bulk of her findings (eighteen versions), however, were what she called "gross tales"—accounts of ordinary people foolishly putting thirteen pet cats, two wet dogs, and two damp human

63

heads of hair into home microwave ovens to be dried, but instead to be cooked or exploded. (The eighteenth version, volunteered by her informant after he heard another of the microwave legends, concerned a cat that was put by a precocious toddler into a trash compacter with a faulty key-lock system.) In most of her stories the pet is wet from a rain shower, a bath, or an accidental dowsing with a hose; the helpful human is either a child (usually a boy) or an older woman. Informants claimed to have heard the stories from a few months to eight years earlier, and they mentioned news reports, as well as other oral accounts, "like the kid putting his cat in the washing machine and that kind of stuff." Both dog versions collected in Salt Lake City concerned poodles being bathed, one in New York and the other in California. The first text mentioned a transition from older to newer appliances:

> Sherrie . . . from Long Island, New York, told this story when there was lull in the conversation. . . . She heard about a lady who had poodles, and she always dried out her poodles in her [conventional] oven. Then she got a microwave, and so she tried to dry her poodles in the microwave; and, of course, the poodle blew up.

By Spring, 1979, the microwave-oven pet tragedy was becoming extremely well known, as folklorist Betty Jane Belanus found in her research. Her first examples of the story came from acquaintances in Toledo, Ohio, and Washington, D.C., both of whom remembered that a newly-washed poodle had been killed by the dangerous waves. Other midwestern versions assembled by Belanus described a dampened cat as often as a wet poodle being the victim. Again, newspaper reports or occasionally children's science or home economics teachers were the supposed sources for the tradition. Related details that Belanus collected were that a live animal's blood will boil in a microwave oven, that scientists use microwaves to kill laboratory animals, and that radiations from television sets are nearly as dangerous to the human body as microwaves. (Microwaves, it should be noted, actually do pose certain dangers to living creatures.)

"THE HIPPIE BABY-SITTER"

The warnings in several "Hot Dog!" texts of the dangers to human beings of mishandling microwave ovens is a theme shared by another urban legend of this story cycle: the hippie baby-sitter who cooks alive a child placed in her care. Here we also see the influence of other baby-sitter scare-stories as well as of the numerous traditions discussed in Chapter 4 about unlikely creatures found in unexpected places. Folklorist Lydia Fish of the State University College in Buffalo, New York, took the first official scholarly notice in the United States of "The Hippie Baby-sitter" in 1971 when she inserted a request for versions of the story in a folklore journal. While she never received any folklorists' replies she did collect many examples from her own students. In the usual versions current in Buffalo, a somewhat freaky-looking baby-sitter is hired, often one who is previously unknown to the parents (or else new parents are leaving the baby with a sitter for the first time). The sitter gets high on marijuana (or LSD, or even Scotch) and cooks the "turkey," that is, the baby, in the oven. A typical New York state text:

> This couple with a teenage son and a little baby left the baby with this hippie-type girl who was a friend of the son's. They went to a dinner party or something, and the mother called in the middle of the evening to see if everything was all right.
> "Sure," the girl says. "Everything's fine. I just stuffed the turkey and put it in the oven."
> Well, the lady couldn't remember having a turkey, so she figured something was wrong. She and her husband went home, and they found that the girl had stuffed the

baby and put it in the oven. Now the son used a lot of drugs, and this girl was a friend of his, so I guess they figure she took them too. . . . This is a true story. We had a meeting at school, and this psychologist told the story. I think he said that it happened to a friend's neighbor.

In Professor Fish's 1971 versions the turkey/baby is usually cooked to death before the parents arrive home, although in a few accounts they come back just in time to save their unlucky infant. In all but one version the sitter is thought or proved to be under the influence of drugs; the exception is a text from Binghamton, New York in which she is simply driven out of her mind by the child's behavior:

> After the parents left, the baby started crying. No matter what the sitter did, the baby would not stop. After a time, the baby's crying drove the sitter mad, and she put the kid in the oven and turned it up as high as it would go.

"The Hippie Baby-sitter" has developed along much the same lines across the country, as well as in Canada, as this Toronto version from 1973 illustrates:

> This story was told to me by a friend who heard it on the news on the radio a year or so ago. It is a factual account.
>
> There was a girl and she was baby-sitting. The parents had gone out to a very big party and had left this infant at home with this sixteen-year-old girl. So she was baby-sitting and they phoned just to see if everything was all right. She said, "Oh, fine. Everything's great. The turkey's in the oven." The mother went, "Oh, okay, fine," and she hung up. Then she looked at her husband and went, "The turkey's in the oven? We didn't have a turkey!" He said, "What's the matter?" So they decided they had better go home and see what was the matter. Maybe there was something wrong with the baby-sitter.
>
> They excused themselves from the party and went home.

So they walked in the house and saw the baby-sitter sitting in the chair freaking out. She had put the little infant in the oven and had thought it was a turkey.

Two versions from the Brigham Young University folklore archive (Provo, Utah) give other details; in one the sitter reports to the parents that "your *roast* is done," and in the other the grim homecoming is described this way:

> When they arrived home, they could smell this awful sickening sweet smell. The mother rushed into the kitchen. There she found the table set for two with her best china and crystal. The lights were out and there were lit candles on the table. In the oven was their baby. The girl had roasted the baby! She said, "Look, I fixed a special dinner for you."

These Brigham Young University versions (1972, 1977) were both, of course, said to be absolutely true. One storyteller commented, however, "If that's true, I'm sick . . . but like I said, that was told from a reliable source." (It was a relative of a friend of a friend, as usual.)

Versions of "The Hippie Baby-sitter" have been collected in Europe, particularly in Scandinavia, sometimes citing an American locale. The earlier occurrence of themes of infanticide in Europe probably explains why his particular modern legend has been so readily accepted there. For instance, in 1972 a Bergen, Norway, newspaper reported a "terror-tale" (*skrekkhistorie*) that shared some specific motifs of "The Hippie Baby-sitter." A couple just departing for a long overseas vacation leave their infant strapped into a highchair in readiness for the baby-sitter's expected arrival in a few minutes. But in different versions the sitter either dies suddenly, suffers an accident on the way there, or simply cannot get into the locked house and thinks the couple has taken the child along with them after all. Upon the parents' return, the baby is found still strapped in the chair where she has starved to death many days before. In this story the direct moral lesson, applicable to either parents or baby-sitters, is very clear, and the theme of the abandoned child (also found in Hansel and Gretel, for example) suggests a deeper level of aggression towards the baby.

The same gruesome tale about an untrustworthy baby-sitter has also circulated in a fully-localized form in Africa, as reported in 1979 by my folklore student Atim Eyere of Calabar, Nigeria. In 1976, Mrs. Eyere remembered, this terrible story swept through the government office where she was working:

> A certain lady who was working in the Ministry of Agriculture called her baby-sitter by telephone to see how her baby was doing. When her baby-sitter told her that the baby was still in bed, she asked her to take him out of bed and sit him up. The words in Efik—*men eyen oro k'etem*—could mean two things, either "sit the baby up" or "cook the baby." So the baby-sitter, being a novice, took this baby and put him in the oven and roasted him. When the mother returned from work, she met the baby-sitter's eyes reddened like the setting sun. The mother said, "Come on, don't be so miserable about nothing. Please bring me my baby."
>
> The baby-sitter, very silent, moved reluctantly to the oven and opened it, and behold the baby was stiff dead in the oven! "Wasn't that what you wanted?" With that she stepped out in a hurry, back to her house, leaving the mother of the baby with wild eyes, crying "My son? Dead?"

Mrs. Eyere was told that the incident happened on Afokang Street, so she asked a friend who lived there about the story. "Oh, no," she answered, "It was along Mayne Avenue." And, Mrs. Eyere told me, "for a few days the news kept traveling until it was all said to have really happened in a neighboring town."

Whether "The Hippie Baby-sitter" has been a direct influence on the "Hot Dog" story or not, the convergence of the two legends occurred recently with the appearance of versions in oral tradition in which the hippie sitter puts the turkey/baby into a microwave oven. Evidently this version has been around for some time too, for a friend of mine who demonstrated microwave ovens when they were first introduced in the United States told me that many people had asked her "What would happen if someone put a cat or a baby into a microwave oven and turned it on?" My friend commented, "I don't know why anyone would think of such a thing, it's so ghoulish." Most likely, they did not think of it themselves at all, but were trying to check on a strange story they had heard or read, about a little boy and his wet cat, an old lady and her poodle, or a freaked-out sitter and her infant charge. These stories answer the question "What would happen if . . ." with the assertion, "Well, this is what *did* happen once. . . ."

Some other cycles of horror stories in American folk tradition, as we have seen, warned against criminal or insane human antagonists. These newer legends reflect fears based on contemporary, often technological, threats while retaining reminders of earlier folkloric themes of child abandonment and infanticide. Given the persistence of such themes, and the current wide acceptance of microwave ovens despite their potential dangers, it seems predictable that such legends as "Hot Dog!" and microwave versions of "The Hippie Baby-sitter" would eventually develop to trouble the dreams of contemporary parents and children.

NOTES

"The Hook"

My students who contributed versions of "The Hook" were Nancy A. Schlehuber (Winter 1978, from Kansas), Laura Fife (Fall 1971, from Albuquerque, New Mexico), and Kathy Arnold (Fall, 1967, from Salt Lake City). An Oregon text appeared in Suzi Jones, *Oregon Folklore* (Eugene: University of Oregon and The Oregon Arts Commission, 1977), p. 65; it was told by a priest and teacher in Portland, perhaps as a warning to his students.

THE VANISHING HITCHHIKER

"The Boyfriend's Death," "The Hook," and similar local traditions were included in Joel D. Rudinger's study of midwestern folk narratives, "Folk Ogres of the Firelands: Narrative Variations of a North Central Ohio Community," *Indiana Folklore*, 9 (1976), 41–93.

John W. Roberts provided an example of "The Hook" merged with a Southwest Missouri legend in his article "The 'Spook Light': A Missouri Parking Legend," in *MidAmerica Folklore*, 7 (1979), 31–40. Linda Dégh's survey of "The Hook" appeared in *Indiana Folklore*, 1 (1968), 92–100. M. E. Kerr's *Dinky Hocker Shoots Smack!* was a paperback published by Dell (New York, 1972); the quoted passage is on page 130. Another literary treatment of "The Hook" was in Jayne Anne Phillips' *Black Tickets* (New York: Dell/Seymour Laurence paperback, 1979), pp. 29–30. Alan Dundes' interpretation of "The Hook" is in his essay "On the Psychology of Legend" in Wayland D. Hand, ed., *American Folk Legend: A Symposium* (Berkeley and Los Angeles: University of California Press, 1971), pp. 21–36. Other published versions are indicated below in connection with the sources of specific legend texts quoted in this chapter.

"The Killer in the Backseat"

Mercyl Alkire, a student of mine in Summer 1967, provided the quoted version of "The Killer in the Backseat." Carlos Drake first published the legend, using the same title, in *Indiana Folklore*, 1 (1968), 107–109; he had three variants. Xenia E. Cord provided eighteen further texts and suggested calling it "The Assailant in the Back Seat" in her article published in *Indiana Folklore*, 2 (1969), 47–54.

"The Baby-sitter and the Man Upstairs"

The Canadian version of "The Baby-sitter and the Man Upstairs" was in Susan Smith's "Urban Tales" in Edith Fowke, ed., *Folklore of Canada* (Toronto: McClelland and Stewart, 1976), p. 264; this source also contained an example of "The Hook" on p. 263. The Texas example of this legend is in Danielle Roemer, "Scary Story Legends," *Folklore Annual*, 3 (1971), 15–16; this source also contained a text of "The Hook" on p. 13. Sylvia Grider provided Indiana University versions of both "The Baby-sitter and the Man Upstairs" and "The Roommate's Death" in her fine analysis of folk legend performance titled "Dormitory Legend-

Telling in Progress: Fall, 1971–Winter, 1973," *Indiana Folklore,* 6 (1973), 1–32.

Sue Samuelson's interpretation of "The Baby-sitter and the Man Upstairs" appeared in her paper titled "The Man Upstairs: An Analysis of Role Models and Sexuality in a Baby-sitting Legend" delivered at the 1978 Annual Meeting of the American Folklore Society in Salt Lake City, Utah, on Friday, October 13th. Samuelson has also found European versions of the legend which she is now studying. The Arizona story about the child hoaxing his baby-sitter was published in *Southwest Folklore,* 3 (Winter, 1979), 1–2, by Keith Cunningham who got it from a Northern Arizona University student of his in Flagstaff. The 1979 Columbia Pictures release *When a Stranger Calls* (directed by Fred Walton and starring Charles Durning, Carol Kane, and Colleen Dewhurst) closely followed "The Baby-sitter and the Man Upstairs" legend. The advertising blurbs said, "Every baby-sitter's nightmare becomes real. . . ." Larry Danielson mentioned *When a Stranger Calls* (footnote 19) and discussed a number of other legend influences in "popular cinematic art" in a film review published in *Western Folklore,* 38 (1979), 209–219. He referred to motifs in sections Z500–599, "Horror Stories," in Ernest W. Baughman's *Type and Motif Index of the Folktales of England and North America* (Indiana University Folklore Series, no. 20, The Hague: Mouton, 1966), but none of the items Baughman listed there are urban legends of much recent currency. This *is,* however, a possible place to index several legends discussed in this book, should any folklorist wish to do so.

"The Roommate's Death"

The Kansas version of "The Roommate's Death" quoted is from Daniel R. Barnes, "Some Functional Horror Stories on the Kansas University Campus," *Southern Folklore Quarterly,* 30 (1966), 305–312, with this legend in particular discussed on pp. 307–308. The California story combining "The Baby-sitter and the Man Upstairs" with "The Roommate's Death" was sent to me by folklorist W. K. McNeil who is gathering material for a study of baby-sitter legends. Linda Dégh's "The Roommate's Death and Related Dormitory Stories in Formation" is in *Indiana Folklore,* 2 (1969), 55–74; she also discussed a group of related rumors and news stories. The analysis by Beverly Crane is "The Structure of Value in 'The Roommate's Death': A Methodology for Interpretive Analysis of Folk Legends," in *Journal of the Folklore Institute,*

14 (1977), 133–149. Her quoted conclusion is on page 147. Another analytic essay making use of this legend is Robert Jerome Smith's "The Structure of Esthetic Response," *Journal of American Folklore,* 84 (1971), 68–79.

Versions of several of these stories appeared in George G. Carey's chapter "Urban and Modern Legends" in *Maryland Folk Legends and Folk Songs* (Cambridge, Maryland: Tidewater Publishers, 1971), pp. 71–87, and in Jo Ann Stephens Parochetti, "Scary Stories from Purdue," *Keystone Folklore Quarterly,* 10 (1965), 49–57.

Alan Dundes' "Metafolklore and Oral Literary Criticism" first published in *The Monist,* 50 (1966), was reprinted in Jan Harold Brunvand, ed. *Readings in American Folklore* (New York: W. W. Norton, 1979), pp. 404–415.

"The Pet (or Baby) in the Oven"

Keith Cunningham's "Hot Dog!" note appeared on pages 27 to 28 of *Southwest Folklore,* 3 (Winter, 1979). Nancy Schlehuber's paper for my class, "Microwave Oven Tales," was written in May, 1978, and Betty Jane Belanus kindly sent me a copy of her Indiana University folklore paper "The Poodle in the Microwave Oven: Free Association and a Modern Legend" dated 18 April 1979.

The query from Lydia Fish about "The Hippie Baby-sitter" appeared in *Folklore Forum,* 6 (1971), 151. Professor Fish sent me copies of several versions collected by her students, and I have quoted from papers written by William J. Kreidler and Janet Hilinski. The Toronto version appeared in Susan Smith's chapter "Urban Tales," in Edith Fowke's *Folklore of Canada* (Toronto: McClelland and Stewart, 1976), p. 265, "Babysitter Mistakes Child for Turkey."

Versions from the Brigham Young University folklore archive were sent to me by Professor William A. Wilson; I quoted texts collected by Pennie Brunson (1972) and Marlene Joyner (1977). The Norwegian account of the trapped baby starving to death was mentioned in the article by Reimund Kvideland concerning "The Solid Cement Cadillac" cited below in Chapter 6; on page 9 Kvideland quotes it from *Bergens Tidende* for September 22, 1972.

Mrs. Atim Eyere reacted with shocked surprise at my telling "The Hippie Baby-sitter" in class during Fall Quarter, 1979; then she wrote out for me the version quoted here as she had heard it three years previously in Nigeria. The *Motif-Index* lists one item that may have a bearing on early or native versions of "The Hippie Baby-sitter"—K1461. *Caring for the child: child killed*—although only a Finnish runic text and a South American myth are cited.

Food writer and consultant Cynthia Scheer transmitted to me in a letter dated September 19, 1979, her memories of and reactions to microwave horror stories heard while she was demonstrating such ovens several years before.

Questions about the history and meaning of the cooked baby legend are far from being finally answered. Suggesting broader distribution and meaning for the story than folklorists have previously suspected, Latin American folklorist Paulo de Carvalho-Neto touched on an apparent Brazilian prototype for the story in his book *Folklore and Psychoanalysis* (Coral Gables, Florida: University of Miami Press, 1972), pp. 42–44. He quoted a "pathological case" described in Marie Langer's study of the Evil Mother theme—*Maternidad y sexo* (Buenos Aires, 1951)—in which a baby left in the care of a servant is roasted and served to the parents upon their return. However, since this "case" was also referred to as "one version," the suspicion arises that we are dealing with folklore rather than actual deviant behavior. Nevertheless, as these psychoanalytic folklorists insist, there are some important links between modern legend, ancient folk themes, and psychology here that deserve closer study. At any rate, the distribution of the cooked baby story is doubtless more extensive in time and space than we can now demonstrate.

4 | Dreadful Contaminations

The Horrendous-Discovery Theme

Americans, on the whole, are a clean people with a low tolerance for unhygienic conditions, especially in their food, persons, or homes. Yet, as much as they despise the company of germs and vermin, some of their folklore depicts the penetration of these creepy invaders to the very heart of their sterile sanctuaries. Cockroaches, spiders, rats, snakes and other reptiles—even relatively harmless ants and mice—all find their places in an urban lore of infestation and contamination. (In a similar vein, school children delight in telling stomach-turning "gross-out" folk stories and parodies, perhaps in part as a maturity rite.)

These dirty interlopers may be one contemporary substitute for the ghosts and ogres of past legends, or possibly a more realistic treatment of the maniac-killer motif in the teenage horror stories. The point of urban legends concerning contamination, somewhat like that of the other scare stories, is revelation of a world of shocking ugliness lying just beneath a surface of tranquility and apparent wholesomeness. Things are not at all what they seem. American adolescents are among the most prolific sources and subjects of such urban legends, as this next example shows.

THE VANISHING HITCHHIKER

"The Spider in the Hairdo"

Esquire magazine published the following chilling story in March, 1976, as an example of teenage "Folklore from the Fifties," for the benefit of "today's generation of teenagers" who presumably lack suitable moral fables to guide them:

THE GIRL WITH THE BEEHIVE HAIRDO
(*Origin: Unknown*)

A girl managed to wrap her hair into a perfect beehive. Proud of her accomplishment, she kept spraying it and spraying it, never bothering to wash it again. Bugs began to live in her hair. After about six months, they ate through to her brain and killed her.

MORAL: wash your hair or die.

The beehive style seems to date the story to the 1950s, although folklorists were not collecting it as much then as in the next two decades. One reason for this is that the story often occurs only as a brief rumor rather than a fully-developed legend. Another is that few folklorists looked at the traditions of high school and college students before the 1960s. But the "Bugs" or (most commonly) "*Spider* in the Hairdo" legend has been well known at least since the 1950s.

Folklorist Barre Toelken in 1968 described the legend's usual adaptation as a piece of modern academic folklore:

> . . . the high school girl . . . keeps passing out in class (usually a class attended by a friend of the narrator) and is finally taken to the hospital in a coma. There a small spider is seen darting into her highly lacquered bouffant hair-do, and the nurses pursue it, only to find a whole nest of black widow spiders in the girl's hair, which, of course, was hospitable to them because it had never been combed for a year. In some versions she recovers, in others she dies, but the tale is so seriously told and received that

students now report having heard the tale told by a teacher (usually a girls' gym instructor or a Health and Hygiene professor) as a true story of what can happen to a girl who does not regularly comb her hair.

Since beehive hairdos are pretty much passé now, today's students tend either to project the story back in time to their high school days, or attribute the event to some middle-aged woman wearing an outdated style. On the other hand, the "Spider in the Hairdo" legend continues to fit into Utah folklore, although often it is merely alluded to: "There was this lady who had her hair done and she didn't want to ruin it, so she didn't wash it for a long time and a black widow spider built a nest in it and bit her and she died." A longer version from a University of Maryland student shows a more typical narrative development and regional adaptation:

When I was fifteen or sixteen years old, bouffant hair styles were very much the rage. It was almost as if it were a contest to see which girl could rat her hair the highest and pour the most hair spray on it. One day I went to the beauty shop to have my hair done. My hairdresser told me this story, and she swore that it really happened to a friend of her niece's.

There was this girl who had ratted her hair so high, and put so much hair spray on it, that she never took it down and combed it out or washed it. One day a spider fell into her hair. When the baby black widow spiders hatched, they bit her scalp and she died. I heard this story all over northern and southern California. When I moved to Baltimore, I met people who had heard the same story. They said it happened to a girl who had been a dancer on the Buddy Dean Show, on Baltimore television. These people said that a bee had gotten into the girl's head and stung her and she died from the bee sting because the doctors couldn't get to her head in time, due to her hair.

While a bee fits the hairdo's usual name best, a black widow spider is a more plausible infester, since bees live in large swarms, fly in and out on various errands, and their stings are not fatal, except to the bee itself and to certain highly-susceptible individuals. One can easily imagine a development from bee to "bug" and finally to the very lethal black widow spider as the story spread. Simply the term "beehive" (perhaps augmented by the expression "to rat" one's hair) might have been enough to suggest the legend's basis to some creative storyteller in the first place. (Another possibility is that insects actually have infested such hairdos, and the facts about such incidents have passed into oral tradition and been modified.) However, a similar story involving a vain woman, her hair, and a spider exists in the *exempla* literature (stories used to illustrate moral points in sermons) of thirteenth-century England. Here is a version of it from the *Speculum Laicorum* [Mirror (i.e., example) for the Laity] as described by a historian of medieval religion:

> There is a sermon story of a certain lady of Eynesham, in Oxfordshire, "who took so long over the adornment of her hair that she used to arrive at church barely before the end of Mass." One day "the devil descended upon her head in the form of a spider, gripping with its legs," until she well-nigh died of fright. Nothing would remove the offending insect, neither prayer, nor exorcism, nor holy water, until the local abbot displayed the holy sacrament before it.

Medievalist Shirley Marchalonis, who recounted this and two similar stories, noted how "cleanliness has replaced godliness as the operative force." She further commented that "The high school girl with the nest of spiders in her hair offends contemporary standards of behavior just as the proud medieval ladies offended contemporary belief. In both cases the story acts as warning and example." While the two stories are similar in plot, it seems highly unlikely that they are actually related historically.

While some people who tell "The Spider in the Hairdo"

(such as the hairdresser in the Maryland version) say they believe it, most seem to accept its warning without being concerned about questioning its truth. As one of my students reported, "I have heard this countless times in one form or another, but always told facetiously." Another recognized the traditional nature of the legend's circulation, saying, "This was going around when I was in high school, and I heard the same story from my little brother who now is in high school." But at least one author seems to have taken the story seriously. Kathrin Perutz wrote in her book *Beyond the Looking Glass: America's Beauty Culture* (1970):

> A few years ago, a girl died mysteriously. After her death, it was discovered she had a nest of spiders in her hair and had died of spiders' bites. Her hair, in emulation of the bouffant look, had been teased and sprayed daily and not washed for many months, to keep the effect.

Even though American folklorists have quoted texts of "The Spider in the Hairdo" in their fieldwork reports and studies only infrequently, Western Kentucky State College folklorist Kenneth Clarke felt that it was well enough known in tradition to serve as the vehicle of satire of folkloristic methods. He dubbed his analysis "a Joco-Serious Inquiry into Folklore Theory from the Psychoanalytical School to the Modern Structuralists." Clarke's sample version of the legend, collected from a midwestern university student, went like this:

> Well, the way I heard it was that this girl . . . had a high hairdo, a balloon. You know—the kind you have to spray all the time to keep up. Anyway, this girl was sitting in class one day at school and the teacher happened to notice that blood was running down the girl's neck, so she asked what was wrong. The girl said nothing was wrong, so I guess she didn't feel anything. But then she fainted, and they had to take her to the hospital.
>
> Well, the way it turned out, the girl died. It seems that she had put so much spray on her hair to keep it

up that it just stayed up all the time, didn't get washed or anything. Finally it got so dirty that it got cockroaches in it. They had eaten a hole right through her head and into her brain.

It really happened, you know; my boy friend read about it in the [Louisville, Ky.] *Courier-Journal* last winter.

Clarke's satirical method was rather heavy-handed, and this sort of thing is probably best appreciated in the original. I will merely report here that the hairdo was shown to be both phallic and womb-like, and the particular insect described was subjected to ingenious tinkerings with the two parts of its name, "cock" and "roach." As for the parody of structuralism, suffice it to say that Clarke developed an interpretation reducible to factors he labelled B/O and S/H, or BOSH.

A graphic little story like this—sometimes believed literally—that involves fainting, blood, and death cannot simply be laughed off as bosh, however. Surely it reflects some real concerns of modern folk just as its early counterpart showed the strong religious concerns of medieval people. The warning not to put fashion or vanity above health and common sense is still meaningful, especially to any woman who wears or has worn sprayed hairdos of this kind. Perhaps the story is also a protest against the dictates of fashion themselves.

The legend has developed some gruesome second cousins in oral tradition in which insects infest other parts of the body. In one story a person has a persistent itch under a plaster cast; the horrible cause is finally discovered to be ants or termites which have gotten into the cast and are eating away at the limb. In another story, a little boy suffers a headache so severe that in a mad frenzy he jams a fork into his forehead, releasing a stream of ants which had taken over his sinus cavities. There is also an updated hairdo story which shares the hippie motif with the baby-sitter legend and is popular among rural or small-town people: here a longhaired hippie dies from the bites of a spider lodged in his frizzy hair. Just what he deserves, presumably.

Finally, as if to validate the sexual theme introduced jokingly in Clarke's satire, we have an emerging legend which seems to derive ultimately from "The Spider in the Hairdo," "The Cucumber in the Disco Pants," which I first heard in early summer, 1979. A young man who has fainted in a discotheque is taken to the emergency room of a nearby hospital. There it is discovered that, in order to look sexier than life, he has put a cucumber (in other versions, a sausage) into the crotch of his skin-tight disco pants. The vegetable pressed hard enough against a blood vessel to cut off circulation and cause him to pass out. When the pressure is relieved, he recovers. Ah vanity . . . ah folklore!

"The Kentucky Fried Rat" and Other Nasties

A number of recurrent stories deal with food contamination, always a real possibility, even with our country's strict regulations of quality-control and inspection. In particular, foreign restaurants and fast-food establishments bear the brunt of these negative traditions. The legends are very credible because virtually all Americans eat foreign or assembly-line food fairly often, and it is not at all unlikely that such nourishment could become adulterated or spoiled. (In both kinds of food the seasonings or the mode of preparation could be suspected of covering up the contamination.) Frequently such traditions reach the media, and media reports—themselves usually unreliable—in turn feed back into folklore. A good example of this occurred recently on America's favorite late-night talk show.

On the evening of May 23, 1979, Johnny Carson told his "Tonight Show" audience about a recent news story concerning a woman who was suing a fast food chain for serving her a "batter-fried rat" instead of fried chicken. He quipped, "It's not the place run by the guy with the white hair and the beard—the trademark of *this* outfit is the Pied Piper . . . they'll ask you, 'Do you want a breast or a tail?' "

There probably *was* such a news story; law suits—and rumors of suits—against food-processing companies for foreign matter found in their products are not uncommon, with rodent parts frequently being involved. Rumors and legends concerning foreign matter in food, nourished, as it were, by the reality, are also common in American folklore, one of the latest and best developed being "The Kentucky Fried Rat" story. Maryland folklorist George G. Carey published this version he had heard in 1971 from a federal employee in Washington, D.C.; the brother-in-law of the narrator said he actually knew a nurse who worked in the hospital mentioned in the story:

> Two couples stopped one night at a notable carry-out for a fried chicken snack. The husband returned to the car with the chicken. While sitting there in the car eating their chicken, his wife said, "My chicken tastes funny." She continued to eat and continued to complain.
>
> After a while the husband said, "Let me see it." The driver of the car decided to cut the light on and then it was discovered that the woman was eating a rodent, nicely floured and fried crisp. The woman went into shock and was rushed to the hospital. It was reported that the husband was approached by lawyers representing the carry-out and offered the sum of $35,000. The woman remained on the critical list for several days. Spokesmen from the hospital would not divulge the facts about the case and nurses were instructed to keep their mouths shut. And it is also reported that a second offer was made for $75,000, and this too was refused. The woman died and presumably the case will come to court.

Expressions in this oral text such as "it was reported" and "presumably" suggest the background of the story in loose, vague, free-floating rumors, perhaps influenced by half-remembered newspaper stories. But the specific setting and dialogue in the tale, the references to the suppression of information, and the exact dollar figures offered to the victims are hallmarks of the full-fledged urban legend. Other versions collected elsewhere offer explanations of the presence of the rat: sickened by a recent poisoning or fumigation of the restaurant it had fallen into the frying batter. This detail may have been borrowed from a much older story in which a visitor to a candy factory sees a rat floating in one of the chocolate vats. Other informants told Carey that the fried rat was first spotted when its tail protruded from one piece of fried "chicken." Eastern lawyers or Justice Department employees, he found, tended to emphasize the legal aspects of the story, while common folk (the rest of us) were more fascinated by the gruesome side of it.

In the versions of "The Kentucky Fried Rat" American teenagers usually tell, the characters are a young couple enjoying a romantic evening before a fireplace. They are having a quiet supper eating their chicken with the lights off and soft music playing. (Dim light is a prerequisite for the woman—seldom is it the man—to eat a few bites of the rat before discovering her awful error.) This setting is analogous to the darkened car of the Washington couple, or a drive-in movie in other texts, and all of these tales remind us of the dating youngsters parked somewhere for petting, with their radio on, in "The Boyfriend's Death" or "The Hook." My own Utah students have told me many local versions of this story, and some have claimed they have been told it had occurred as far away as Alabama.

There is a rather well-known European tradition of the restaurant rat story, frequently reported in the press there, which is possibly the prototype of "The Kentucky Fried Rat" legend in the United States. In the British Isles the tradition tends to concern a rat bone found in food served at a Chinese restaurant, but sometimes the contaminant is dog meat (frequently of "Alsatians," that is, German shepherds). One Swedish report of the story (among many that exist) placed it in Greece. On October 29, 1973, the Stockholm newspaper *Dagens*

Nyheter published a story about a man from Norrköping, Sweden, who had vacationed on the Greek island of Rhodes. He had enjoyed a wonderful lunch of chicken salad there, but had the bad luck to get a bone stuck in his throat. His doctor in Sweden removed the bone, which he recognized at once as a bone from a rat rather than a chicken. A subsequent investigation uncovered a freezer full of rats in the back room of the Rhodes restaurant.

Folklorist Donald Ward has compared the typical West German and American versions of the story. In Germany the legend usually concerns a small privately-owned foreign restaurant (often Yugoslavian), and the food contamination is both intentional and malicious. In the United States the food in the story is contaminated accidentally by employees of "an impersonal corporate chain." Thus, the German stories warn against supposed unsanitary and dishonest foreign workers, while the American tradition criticizes the impersonality and carelessness of big business.

Gary Alan Fine of the University of Minnesota recently analyzed 115 versions of "The Kentucky Fried Rat," finding such textual variations as fried-rat pranks perpetrated by disgruntled fast-food workers, fried mouse and cat stories, and the idea that the blend of spices in the fried-chicken batter was developed to mask the rat flavor. Observing that the victim is always a woman, Fine suggested that "by neglecting her traditional role as food preparer [she] helps to destroy the family by permitting the transfer of control from the home to amoral profit-making corporations. . . . the rat is appropriate symbolic punishment." One text collected by Fine which beautifully supported this reading describes a wife "who didn't have anything ready for supper." She attempts to pass off commercial fried chicken as her own cooking by serving it to her husband by candlelight. The meal is a travesty of "home cooking," and the wife, of course, in the dim light, gets the piece of fried rat in return for her duplicity.

The all-time favorite story about food contamination involves

Dreadful Contaminations

a nasty rodent, or part of one, found in a soft-drink bottle. I first encountered it as a mouse tail in a Pepsi Cola bottle, but the variations are numerous. Folklorists have long regarded such stories as merely evidence of untrustworthy "Cokelore," but a recent study turned up numerous actual court cases involving such claims. Gary Alan Fine, a tireless urban legend scholar, made a systematic search of published state appellate court records. He reasoned that actual events might very well underlie the almost invariable references by the tellers of mouse-in-coke stories to news stories, court cases, or both. In fact, most first-year law students study such cases, and George Carey had already called folklorists' attention to one such report of an actual case from the *Washington Post*, February 3, 1971:

> A 76-year-old Falls Church man was awarded $20,000 in damages yesterday on his claim that he was "permanently sickened" by drinking a bottle of Coca-Cola that contained part of a mouse.
>
> George Petalas was awarded the settlement by a Fairfax County Circuit Court jury, which debated for two hours.
>
> In his suit, Petalas claimed that he bought a 10-cent bottle of Coca-Cola on March 20, 1969 from a vending machine in a Safeway Store at 3109 Graham Rd., Falls Church.
>
> He took two swallows in the presence of a store employee, William Wheeler, Petalas said, when he noticed "a strange taste." He and Wheeler then went outside the store and poured the rest of the bottle on a driveway, Petalas testified. At the bottom, Petalas contended, were the back legs and tail of a mouse.
>
> Petalas was hospitalized for three days at Arlington Hospital following the incident, he testified. He alleged through his attorney, Robert J. Arthur, that he has since been unable to eat meat, and has lived on a diet of grilled cheese, toast and noodles.
>
> Petalas, who lives at 4418 Duncan Drive, Falls Church,

asked $100,000 in damages from the two defendants, Safeway Stores, Inc. and the Coca-Cola Bottling Company of Alexandria. According to Arthur the money represented medical expenses and "past and future mental anguish."

According to the presiding judge, Albert V. Bryan, Jr., the bottling company's defense was that the mouse could only have gotten into the bottle through "tampering."

Doubtless many similar news items have been published, but since most newspapers are not indexed and as easily accessible after their initial circulation as the court appeals records, their exact influence on oral tradition is difficult to gauge. In other words, the mouse-in-coke legend may have its origin in actual events, but it is impossible to say exactly *how* this occurred. The kinds of details, such as darkness and the result of the discovery of the contamination of food, that have entered into court cases and could have fed into oral legends either directly or via the press are suggested in this portion of another case report quoted by Professor Fine:

> The plaintiff, Ella Reid Creech, lives about a quarter of a mile from this store [where the Coca-Cola was purchased] and about 6 p.m. on the date last named [January 9, 1931] sent her sister Tillie to this store to get her two bottles of Coca-Cola. She got them and handed one to the plaintiff. The room was dark. Plaintiff opened the bottle and drank it. She became very sick and began to vomit. A light was turned on and she discovered a partially decomposed mouse in the bottle. Dr. Darnell was called and pumped and washed out her stomach. (Coca-Cola Bottling Co., of Shelbyville [Ky.] v. Creech, 53 S.W. 2d 745)

The earliest case that Fine located was brought in Mississippi by one Harry Chapman against the Jackson Coca-Cola Bottling Co. The company appealed the decision against them in 1914, but the lower court ruling was affirmed. The presiding judge, quoting from Robert Burns's famous poem "To a

Mouse," poetically remarked "A 'sma' mousie' caused the trouble in this case. The 'wee, sleekit, cow'rin' tim'rous beastie' drowned in a bottle of Coca-Cola." Thereafter, forty-four further cases were appealed up to 1976, but (since records are not published of trial court proceedings) no one can say how many cases were originally brought without their decisions being appealed, nor how many suits were settled out of court. The plaintiffs in the appeals, unlike the typical characters of the legend versions, were more often men than women (twenty-five versus twenty). The cases occurred in twenty-three states and the District of Columbia, and in every decade since 1914, with the largest number (fifteen) happening in the 1950s, and the greatest regional concentration (twenty-one) in the southern states.

Undoubtedly, the constant recurrence of contamination suits in all parts of the country could not help but keep the urban legends of mouse parts in food and drink alive; conversely, it is not out of the question that some of the cases may have been falsified as a result of knowledge of the legends. One could also speculate that disgruntled company employees who know the stories decide to prove them true by sabotaging the soft-drink bottles. Can it be only coincidence that mice are so often the animals involved and that they find their way specifically into soft-drink bottles? Professor Fine's forty-five cases all dealt with mice in soda bottles, but he also uncovered other suits in which cockroaches, maggots, worms, putrid peanuts, cigarette butts, kerosene, concrete, glass slivers, hairpins, safety pins, paint, and a condom were found variously in milk cartons, beer bottles, pies, and in dishes served in Chinese restaurants. Nevertheless, the majority of *oral legends* deal with mouse parts in soft drinks.

The possible transmutation of facts into folklore may be shown by comparing two more of Professor Fine's examples with oral legend texts. First, here is a case quoted from a court record in the typical straightforward, unemotional style of such documents:

87

THE VANISHING HITCHHIKER

On the night of July 24, 1943, plaintiff and her sister went to the Spa Sweet Shop, sat at the counter and each ordered a bottle of Coca-Cola. The waitress took two bottles of Coca-Cola from the cooler, removed the caps therefrom with a bottle opener and placed one bottle in front of plaintiff and one in front of her sister. Plaintiff placed a straw in each bottle and without looking particularly at the contents of her bottle she proceeded to drink same through the straw. According to plaintiff, the following then occurred: "When I got half way down, I remarked to my sister, 'It had an awful taste to it.' She said hers was all right. I kept on drinking, and when I came to the bottom of the bottle, the straw hit something. I picked up the bottle and looked at it, and there was a mouse in it. ***I let out a scream, and the owner came up and told me to keep quiet, not to attract too much attention on account he had a few customers in the store***. I got nauseated, and I went on out and threw up." (Patargias v. Coca-Cola Bottling Co. of Chicago, Inc., 74 N.E. 2d 162)

Compare this account to the following urban legend that was collected some thirty years later by Fine from a student at the University of Minnesota:

Two old ladies stopped into a restaurant to have a little lunch and they both sat down and made their orders and ordered Seven-Up. It came in the old green bottles. And they were sitting there and each poured themselves a glass, and they were chatting away as usual like old ladies do, and uh . . . and they finished their first glass and one of them was pouring a second glass of Seven-Up, and all of a sudden she noticed something kinda toward the bottom of the bottle, and she just couldn't quite make out what it was, so they started looking at it, trying to figure out what this thing was at the bottom of the Seven-Up bottle, and finally they tried to pour it out and it came out and it was a decomposed mouse, and they both fainted and they were both revived later on, and after they got

88

home they sued the Seven-Up company, and they made thousands of dollars on the lawsuit. (Tape transcription collected from L. H., November 15, 1976, white male, mid-twenties, in Minneapolis; heard from male friends in Davenport, Iowa, ca. 1960–1965, believed as true.)

The process of legend formation going on here is not simply the retelling of a news account in garbled form; the Minnesota storyteller could not have reworked elements from the court case, since he himself did not know about it. Rather, the multiple cross-influence of folklore with court testimony and the news media is to be suspected, with the folk raconteur usually making a better tale of it than either lawyers or journalists. Storytellers somewhere up the line may well have read a corroborating news story. It is interesting to note that while oral tradition often states or implies that many thousands of dollars were won in law suits against soft drink bottlers, the actual monetary awards in thirty-five cases reviewed by Professor Fine ranged from $50 to $20,000, with the median award being only $1,000 and the mean $1,727.

Very few—if any—folk informants ever have a news clipping about foreign matter in food to back up their claims that the story they know is a true one. Their "evidence" remains in *oral* tradition. Recent food rumors are usually only summary accounts based on unverifiable descriptions of supposed news stories, and they are thus probably legends in the making. For example, both Pop Rocks (an effervescing-in-the-mouth candy manufactured by General Foods) and Bubble Yum (a chewing gum produced by Life Savers, Inc.) became the subjects of adolescent rumors in 1977. A few Pop Rocks (sometimes an entire package), according to the typical story, were swallowed whole and the internal fizzing killed a child. But informants for the "true" story, which is usually well localized, who claimed to have read it in a newspaper or a magazine never could produce such an article, or they found clippings about only slightly related *general* food concerns. Bubble Yum, according to rumor, either contained spider eggs, caused cancer, or both. While informants insisted they remembered reading about actual cases, the only newspaper stories so far discovered have been reports debunking the rumor itself. Nevertheless, the power of the rumor was so strong that the Life Saver manufacturers felt compelled to run full-page advertisements in the *New York Times* and other publications, headlined "Someone is Telling Your Kids Very Bad Lies about a Very Good Gum."

Most recently, McDonald's Corporation has been the victim of two nationwide rumors. First, early in 1977, the story spread that McDonald's was donating a hefty percentage of its profits to a Satanic cult. That story had barely died down when in late 1978 another one began, claiming that Big Macs were being filled out with worms used as a protein supplement. (Worms, it should be mentioned, cost more per pound than beef. The same may be said about kangaroo meat, also sometimes rumored as a McDonald-burger beef-stretcher.) Neither of these rumors has so far received the dramatic and stylistic narrative treatment characteristic of fully-developed urban legends, but clearly there is some interplay between these American rumors and legends, since both deal with mass-produced, mass-consumed foods that are especially popular with young people. Their message is "Watch what you eat, especially if it comes in a pretty package or from a big fast-food chain."

Incidentally, the deliberate planting of these nasty-food stories by competing food or drink processors is unlikely, since the spread and variation of such stories is unpredictable and a rumor is just as likely to fasten on one company as another. The best defense against nasty-food lore seems to be silence, since eventually the stories fade more or less away, and in the long run they seldom harm a big company.

"Alligators in the Sewers"

The theme of displaced creatures is an old one, and modern folklore has spawned many rumors of an animal—usually a fearsome one—lurking where it does not belong. Sometimes, the storyteller has embroidered a legend around this base of hearsay. Folklorist Patrick Mullen sketched out the process:

". . . individuals try to attribute causes, motives, and reasons, and in so doing they also make the story more plausible. For instance, the traditional legend that there are alligators in the sewers of New York City poses a primary question: how did they get there? One traditional variant provides as a cause that tourists just back from Florida brought live baby alligators with them and tiring of their pets flushed them down the toilets where they proceeded to propagate."

Although few other American folklorists have even mentioned this particular "traditional legend" in print, most of us have heard it, and there are mass media references aplenty to the "Alligators in the Sewers" story which confirm its wide circulation. These sources also show that Mullen's summary represented a standard plot which may be outlined as follows: *Baby Pets* (often from Florida), *Flushed,* then *Grow in Sewers* (usually in New York City). A very straightforward reference by two herpetologists Sherman A. Minton, Jr., and Madge Rutherford Minton in their book *Giant Reptiles* (1973) suggested not only this motif-sequence and the existence of variants, but also a likely date of its popularity:

One of the sillier folktales of the late 1960s was that the New York sewers were becoming infested with alligators, presumably unwanted pets that had been flushed down the toilet. In some of the accounts, these were growing to formidable size from feeding on rats. We have been unsuccessful in tracing the source of these legends but would assure New Yorkers that alligators are not among their urban problems.

For its sophisticated audience the *New Yorker* in 1974 offered this fantasy-parody of the story:

THE VANISHING HITCHHIKER

A FOOLISH LEGEND

The sewers of New York City do not teem with crocodilians that once were house pets, as has often been rumored. Those long, menacing objects are minisubs of uncertain origin, perhaps Bolivian.

A work of serious modern fiction included one of the most detailed versions of the legend. Thomas Pynchon's rather inscrutable 1963 novel *V.* contains this passage, given as the report of a hip Puerto-Rican New York street gang:

> Did he remember the baby alligators? Last year, or maybe the year before, kids all over Nueva York bought these little alligators for pets. Macy's was selling them for fifty cents; every child, it seemed, had to have one. But soon the children grew bored with them. Some set them loose in the streets, but most flushed them down the toilets. And these had grown and reproduced, had fed off rats and sewage, so that now they moved big, blind, albino, all over the sewer system. Down there, God knew how many there were. Some had turned cannibal because in their neighborhood the rats had all been eaten, or had fled in terror.

Although Pynchon wove a surrealistic subterranean fantasy around the theme of alligators living in the sewers—with an Alligator Patrol hired to hunt them down—his treatment of the basic legend is essentially traditional. The details of their turning white and going blind not only correspond to the actual physical development of other animals living for many generations in dark caves, but the albinism has become a standard part of both this legend and the one about "New York White" marijuana, supposedly growing in the city's sewers from all the weed flushed down toilets during drug busts. In his *America in Legend* Richard Dorson published texts including both these New York traditions collected from Berkeley, California, students in the late 1960s. The legendary white weed—white, because of the lack of sunlight—grows lushly in the sewer because of the nutrients; those who would harvest it are deterred, however, because:

> . . . full-grown alligators prowled the sewers of New York. It seems that Miami vacationers returning to New York in the winter brought back baby alligators as pets for their children. The more the alligators grew the less ideal they appeared as playmates, and their owners, too tenderhearted to skin them for their hides, mercifully flushed them down the toilet. Some survived in their new environment and confronted sewer maintenance workers, who publicly protested at this unnecessary additional hazard to their occupation.

A version of the alligator story with the details of whiteness and blindness found in Pynchon's account, was reported as a folk legend in *Psychology Today* in 1975:

> Perhaps you've heard about the blind white alligators that live in the New York sewers. They're the descendants of tiny alligators brought back as souvenirs of Florida vacations. People living in studio apartments didn't know what to do with them, and in desperation flushed them down the toilet. The beasts are white because they don't get any sunlight paddling along under the streets, and blind because it's too dark to see.

Puzzled by the lack of more voluminous folkloristic data on the oral legend which he knew well as a New York City native, University of Utah graduate student Ed D'Alessandro in 1978 collected versions of the rumor and the story from a cross section of other UU students. While his sample was small and the location of the study was far from the streets of Manhattan, D'Allesandro's findings probably represented the current folk tradition fairly well.

Sixteen students he interviewed, ranging in age from nineteen to twenty-seven, knew the story in some form. Seven were from the state of New York (usually New York City); the others from the Midwest or far west, including Salt Lake City.

Nine men and seven women were in the group. All of them knew at least the outline of the story—baby alligator pets, flushed, thrived in sewers. Four identified Florida as the source of the pets, but two believed they had been purchased locally —in a department store or a ball park. Four informants had heard the story "when I was small," but two furnished more specific dates in the late 1950s or mid 1960s. In seven of the sixteen versions New York City was stated or clearly implied as the place where the alligators now lived, but one each reported the Mississippi River, Denver, or Salt Lake City. (There were six accounts with no specified location; New York is the most likely setting for these as well, because Ed D'Alessandro was probably known to the students to be from there, and they may have assumed that *he* knew where the story was native.) Thus, the legend seems to be fairly standardized, but still, in the manner of all folklore, it remains adaptable to different regions and situations.

Two aspects of D'Alessandro's survey are of particular interest in the analysis of rumor and legend. First, five of the informants offered a specific supposed validation for the legend. Three reported that sewer workers had been bitten by alligators. Another said, as a preliminary to telling the legend, that his neighbor had actually flushed his baby pet "alligator" down a toilet when his mother objected to it. A student from New York City said that she had seen an alligator looking up at her through a sewer grating. Second, a substantial number of references were made to media sources to validate the story. Six students insisted they had learned about it in broadcast or printed sources: "adventure/male magazines," *National Lampoon*, a radio program, Johnny Carson, Dick Cavett, "The Honeymooners" (a Jackie Gleason television series in which Art Carney played a sewer worker), and even Pynchon's *V*. Both of these findings help to show the typical growth of legend from a brief original rumor that gradually acquires validating details as it is repeated from person to person, also incorporating mass-media reports (or at least *reports* of such reports).

Conspicuously absent from the sixteen accounts was any mention that the alligators were blind or white, although several students did comment on the ecosystem of sewers, the chances of other flushed pets (such as goldfish) surviving there, and the large size (up to eight feet long) to which they thought alligators might grow in such an environment. One New York City native, without making an explicit reference to Pynchon or other writers, related a communal folk fantasy which included elements similar to those found in various printed accounts:

> One time when my friends and I were hanging out we decided to explain the smoke that comes out of the sewers in the winter. We figured that with all the marijuana that gets flushed, and the fetuses, and the alligators, they all grow, and the babies ride around on the alligators smoking the dope, which grows to be really potent, and that's what that smoke really is.

One is inclined to attribute the origin of "Alligators in the Sewers" stories solely to the imaginations of youths (the most common narrators) contemplating the environment of the sewers, where some of their own reptile pets may have ended up, and improvising further details. Lending credence to the rumor would be personal experiences of pets actually having been flushed away (not alligators, likely, but caimans or other small crocodilians). Having seen in zoos, films, or books how big an alligator might grow, the mind of a young storyteller seems capable of developing the legend, which could then be nourished by published or broadcast references. Another stimulus to such stories is the fact that baby reptiles would eventually become terrible house pets, impossible to train or restrain, expensive to feed, and ultimately (for most people) repulsive to watch. The legend offers a way out of the dilemma.

But *could* there be some truth to the story? People always ask this when it comes up in conversation. Surely the sewers of New York would be much too cold in the winter for tropical reptiles to survive, and the odds seem great against a baby alligator living through both the traumatic experience of the flushing and the dark, fetid environment below. Even if they lived, is there any chance that the babies would find each other in order to mate and multiply, and could they and their eggs avoid the flowing current and the sewage treatment plants at the other end?

No, no, no, all our instincts and our experience with other folk legends tell us: this must be just another false-true tale made believable by the artful narration of realistic details. Nevertheless, there *is* one reliable account of a full-grown alligator dragged from a New York City sewer. It was discovered in the backfiles of the *New York Times* by anthropologist Loren Coleman whose research on "unusual phenomena and events," especially animal lore, eventually resulted in a list of more than seventy reported encounters with alligators in very unexpected places all around the United States from 1843 to 1973. Only one of these reports involved a sewer, however, and that sewer was on East 123rd Street in Manhattan. The *Times* story of February 10, 1935, opened:

ALLIGATOR FOUND IN UPTOWN SEWER

YOUTHS SHOVELING SNOW INTO MANHOLE
SEE THE ANIMAL CHURNING IN ICY WATER

SNARE IT AND DRAG IT OUT

REPTILE SLAIN BY RESCUERS
WHEN IT GETS VICIOUS—
WHENCE IT CAME IS MYSTERY

The youthful residents of East 123rd Street, near the murky Harlem River, were having a rather grand time at dusk yesterday shoveling the last of the recent snow into a gaping manhole.

Salvatore Condulucci, 16 years old, of 419 East 123rd

Street, was assigned to the rim. His comrades would heap blackened slush near him, and he, carefully observing the sewer's capacity, would give the last fine flick to each mound.

Suddenly there were signs of clogging ten feet below, where the manhole drop merged with the dark conduit leading to the river. Salvatore yelled: "Hey, you guys, wait a minute," and got down on his knees to see what was the trouble.

What he saw, in the thickening dusk, almost caused him to topple into the icy cavern. For the jagged surface of the ice blockade below was moving; and something black was breaking through. Salvatore's eyes widened; then he managed to leap to his feet and call his friends.

"Honest, it's an alligator!" he exploded.

The rest of the story, with its sad end for the reptile, is summarized in the headlines. The alligator turned out to be "seven and a half or eight feet" long. And "whence it came?" The reporter suggested maybe a passing boat from—of course— "the mysterious Everglades."

Perhaps, then, Coleman has found the single origin for one of the most enduring urban legends. According to a former New York City Commissioner of Sewers there was a problem with alligators in the sewers in the mid 1930s. In his book on the development of utilities beneath Manhattan Island, titled *The World Beneath the City*, Robert Daley claims that recurrent reports of alligators in the sewers finally forced Sewer Commissioner Teddy May to inspect the situation personally. May told Daley that he *did* find alligators (averaging two-feet long); he immediately launched a campaign to eradicate them, and was able to announce their extermination by 1937. Some of the reports May had heard might have been folklore, of course, and Daley's published account of his interviews (1959) may be one source both of Pynchon's novelistic treatment and of some of the current folk legends. The most important point, however, is that only themes that the collective taste of the folk find appealing will be absorbed into their lore. In other words, "Alligators in the Sewers" fits right in with "The Spider in the Hairdo" and "The Kentucky Fried Rat" in their shared theme of animals contaminating the human environment.

Whatever the origin of the tales, both the intriguing example of dogged survival under adverse conditions and a general fascination with what is "down there" in the sewers are sufficient to keep the story popular. In fact, there was a children's book, and a rather charming one, based on the legend which emphasized these points. Peter Lippman's *The Great Escape, or The Sewer Story* (1973) chronicled the return of New York City's sewer alligators to the Florida swamps by disguising themselves as tourists and chartering a flight from which they bail out over the jungle.

NOTES

"The Spider in the Hairdo"

Gail Parent's feature "Folklore from the Fifties" containing the quoted text of "The Spider in the Hairdo" appeared in *Esquire*, March 1976, pp. 76–77. Barre Toelken discussed this and other urban legends in "The Folklore of Academe" which is Appendix B in Jan Harold Brunvand, *The Study of American Folklore*, 2nd. ed. (New York: W. W. Norton, 1978), pp. 372–390, an essay first published in 1968; the quotation in this chapter appears on p. 377. My students Laura Fife and DeeAnne Ward gave me their versions of the legend, and their comments on them in Fall 1971.

The version from the University of Maryland is in George G. Carey's *Maryland Folk Legends and Folk Songs* (Cambridge, Maryland: Tidewater Publishers, 1971), p. 87. Shirley Marchalonis discussed the medieval *exempla* in her article "Three Medieval Tales and their Modern American Analogues," *Journal of the Folklore Institute*, 13 (1976), 173–184, reprinted in Jan Harold Brunvand, ed., *Readings in American Folklore* (New York: W. W. Norton, 1979), pp. 267–278. She quoted the passage given in this chapter from G. R. Owst, *Preaching in Medieval England* (1926) on p. 268 in the reprint.

Perutz's *Beyond the Looking Glass* (New York: Wm. Morrow, 1970) has the spider story on p. 308. It was reprinted in the consumer newsletter *Moneysworth* on October 4, 1971, according to Ronald L. Baker in "The Influence of Mass Culture on Modern Legends," *Southern Folklore Quarterly*, 40 (1976), 372.

Kenneth Clarke's interpretation appeared as "The Fatal Hairdo and the Emperor's New Clothes Revisited," *Western Folklore*, 23 (1964), 249–252.

"The Kentucky Fried Rat"

George G. Carey's traditional version of "The Kentucky Fried Rat" appeared on page 71 of his *Maryland Folk Legends and Folk Songs* (Cambridge, Maryland: Tidewater Publishers, 1971). On pages 72 to 73 of the same book Carey reprinted the *Washington Post* story about the mouse parts in the Coca-Cola bottle. Various notes and queries in the British folklore journal *Lore and Language* from 1972 to 1978 have described rat-bone stories about restaurants both in Great Britain and on the Continent. The Rhodes-rat story from *Dagens Nyheter* headlined "Rattben i halsen" [Rat bone in the Throat] was sent by Ingemar Liman of Stockholm to Louie W. Attebery, College of Idaho, Caldwell, who then kindly lent it to me. Donald Ward's discussion of "The Kentucky Fried Rat" appears in his article "American and European Narratives as Socio-Psychological Indicators," in *Folk Narrative Research: Some Papers Presented at the VI Congress of the International Society for Folk Narrative Research*, Juha Pentikainen and Tuula Juuvikka, ed., *Studia Fennica*, 20 (Helsinki, 1976), 348–353. Gary Alan Fine kindly sent me a pre-publication copy of his paper "The Kentucky Fried Rat: Legends and Modern Mass Society" (24 pp.) in April, 1980.

The pioneering article on "cokelore" which introduced the term in its title was by L. Michael Bell and published in *Western Folkloke*, 35 (1976), 59–64. It is reprinted in Jan Harold Brunvand, ed., *Readings in American Folklore* (New York: W. W. Norton, 1979), pp. 99–105.

Gary Alan Fine's article "Cokelore and Coke Law: Urban Belief Tales and the Problem of Multiple Origins" appeared in the *Journal of American Folklore*, 92 (1979), 477–482. All of my examples of Professor Fine's texts appeared there. Fine also sent me a copy of his paper read at the 1977 meeting of the American

Folklore Society in Detroit which dealt in part with the Pop Rocks rumor.

An Associated Press story by Malcolm N. Carter which ran in the *Salt Lake Tribune* on November 15, 1978, dealt with various rumors which bedevilled large food processing companies, especially McDonalds and the Satanic-cult story. On the same page the *Tribune* ran a United Press International report on the newer worms-in-the-Big-Mac story. An April 2, 1977, clipping in my files from the *National Observer* dealt with the Bubble Yum rumors and illustrated the *New York Times* advertisement that denied it, as well as quoting two folklorists to the effect that rumors grow mysteriously and die hard. Susan Domowitz reviewed a dozen foreign-matter-in-food legends collected in Michigan between 1948 and 1955 in a note in *Indiana Folklore,* 12 (1979), 86–95.

"Alligators in the Sewers"

I quote Patrick B. Mullen from his article "Modern Legend and Rumor Theory," *Journal of the Folklore Institute,* 9 (1972), 109. Sherman A. Minton, Jr., and Madge Rutherford Minton's book *Giant Reptiles* was published by Scribner's (New York, 1973); the quoted passage is on p. 34. The *New Yorker* example is from Calvin Tomkins' humorous piece "The Crocodile and You" (7 January 1974), p. 27. Pynchon's *V.* was published by Lippincott (Philadelphia and New York, 1963); I quote from pages 42–43, and the Alligator Patrol entered in Chapter 5, especially pages 111–123.

Richard M. Dorson's material on "Alligators in the Sewers" and "New York White" is in *America in Legend* (New York: Pantheon Books, 1973), pp. 291–292. Jack Horn referred to the same two legends in "White Alligators and Republican Cousins—The Stuff of Urban Folklore," a book review in *Psychology Today,* November, 1975, p. 126.

Ed D'Alessandro's study was done as a class project in American Folklore, Spring 1978, and is summarized with his permission. He called my attention to the Tomkins and Pynchon references.

The *New York Times* text discovered by Loren Coleman, and his discussion of it, appeared in a note "Alligators-in-the-Sewers: A Journalistic Origin," *Journal of American Folklore,* 92 (1979), 335–338. Coleman provided the references to Jack Horn and the Mintons' accounts of the legend. In response to Coleman's note, George Fergus called attention to Robert Daley's *The World Be-*

neath the City (Philadelphia and New York: Lippincott, 1959) in a note "More on Alligators in the Sewers," *Journal of American Folklore,* 93 (1980), 182. Daley's account appears in his book on pages 187 to 189.

Lippman's juvenile book *The Great Escape* was published by The Golden Press (New York, 1973; second printing, 1974).

5 | Purloined Corpses and Fear of the Dead

The disposal of unwanted pets is apparently a live concern of legend tellers and their audiences. Overgrown baby alligators may be flushed down into the sewers (see Chapter 4), but what of the presumably more common problem of how to dispose of a *dead* pet? The unfortunate creature is usually a cat in this story cycle, but in several related legends that express a more deep-seated concern about the presence of death in the home, it is a human corpse.

"The Dead Cat in the Package"

Obviously, you cannot flush a cat's body down the toilet, and for an apartment dweller, burying the corpse in the yard is usually out of the question. This is a real and a practical problem, and folklore has come to the rescue with the amazingly long-lived and fluid legend of the late feline companion neatly wrapped for delivery elsewhere. Along the way it is lost or stolen.

I first heard of this story in 1958 when as a graduate student at Indiana University I helped proofread Richard M. Dorson's new book *American Folklore* and encountered a reference to the story in the "Modern Folklore" chapter. The following year a similar version appeared as an authenticated *true* story in the front-page column "Roundin' the Square" in the *Daily Herald-Telephone,* the local Bloomington, Indiana, newspaper (28 May 1959):

> Chamber of Commerce Manager Jules Hendricks tells about a neighbor of his in Indianapolis who found a novel way of disposing of the remains of a dead cat. Knowing the city ordinance prohibited burying the body, the woman called a friend of hers who lived in the country and asked if she would bury the body for her. The friend agreed, and they planned to meet for the exchange at a downtown department store tea room.
>
> Carrying the cat in a brown paper bag, the woman stopped to do some shopping en route to her rendezvous —and carelessly laid the bag on a counter. When she returned, the bag was gone. A clerk sympathized, explaining that the store had been having trouble with shoplifters lately. Her problem solved (if not in the way she had planned), the woman started home.
>
> Just outside the store, she found a crowd of people had gathered. Squeezing among them to find out what the attraction was, she saw the unconscious body of a 200-pound woman, clutching to her breast a brown paper bag from which protruded the head of her dead cat.

I carried the newspaper clipping around for years, using it as a classroom and conversational example of a published urban legend. Eventually someone gave me a 1963 *San Francisco Chronicle* column by Herb Caen about "fables of our time." It turned out that "two of the most durable San Francisco myths [sic] involve cats." We will look at the second one later, but here is Caen's version of the first:

> The Story of the Dead Cat: a woman, for reasons unexplained, places her dead cat in a shoebox and, on the way to bury it, stops in a downtown department store.

(Why?). As she is shopping, she places the box on a counter, and it disappears. A few minutes later, the store detective finds a lady shoplifter passed out in the powder room, the open shoebox on her lap. I first printed that in 1938—it was hoary then—and it reappears in somebody's column at least once a year, as gospel.

It should be noted that the two versions solve the disposal problem for the cat owners, and simultaneously punish the shoplifter, both of whom are always women. Though brief, both stories give a certain amount of detail about the wrapping of the package, the nature of the shoplifter, and the scene of the final discovery. Other versions add plausible details to explain, for example, why the cat owner must put the package down (perhaps to try on some gloves in the store, or to apply makeup). The reference to a city ordinance in the Indiana story adds verisimilitude, but it must be incorrect since pets have to be buried somewhere. What is the significance of the great weight of the female shoplifter, by the way? (Does it merely dramatize the moment when she faints?) We will encounter again the motifs of the department store "tea room" and the cat package on the shoplifter's lap or held to her breast. At any rate, it is certainly clear that no one in the legend is pleased about the presence of the corpse—or even very rational about how to respond to it.

The missing motivation for wanting to transfer the cat's body elsewhere in Caen's version is supplied in another text, published in a mimeographed newsletter called *Arkansas Folklore* in 1953. This time the scene is Washington, D.C., the place a local department store where (of course) it *really* happened:

THE CORPSE OF THE CAT

This lady we knew in Washington was working for the Government and living, as so many government girls do, in a rooming house. She had brought her cat with her when she came, and the cat was pretty old. One day it died, and she didn't know how to dispose of it. So she phoned a friend who lived way out North West, and the friend said to bring it out, and they'd bury it in her garden. (In one version, she suggests a pet cemetery.) So that being her day off, the woman got on the bus with the cat in a shoe-box, and went into town. While changing buses, at E Street, she thought she'd stop into Woodward and Lothrop's to get some things she needed. Which she did. She laid the bundle down on the counter and got the things she needed—the store would be closed by the time she was on her way home—and turned to pick up her cat. But no cat. The clerk asked her what was the matter, and she said she'd lost her bundle. Not knowing whether to laugh or cry, the lady stood dazed there while the clerk called the house detective. That, the detective, a woman in plain clothes, said, was a typical shoplifter's trick to take something from a private person rather then from the department store, which would be more likely to prosecute. She said further that there was a woman whom they'd been watching and that if she knew her she'd take it immediately to the ladies' room where she'd examine her loot and do away with the wrapping in order to disguise it—they all did, all the female shoplifters, that is. So they went up, and waited. The matron finally had to open one of the booths with her key, and there was a woman in a faint with a dead cat in her lap!

The same 1953 publication contained an important second variant of the cat corpse tale. In fact, one essential detail of the story is so different—the cat-package is not shoplifted, but somehow, without the owner's noticing it, a similar package is substituted for it—that it should probably be labelled a different subtype, B. (It converges with Subtype A in the fact that a friend arranges to meet the cat owner.) This story, the collector reported, "a friend of ours tells . . . on herself." The setting here is London, and the single woman is a scholar rather than a government worker:

THE CAT PARCEL

She is a maiden-lady scholar and was working at the British Museum. Living in a boarding house, she was unable to keep a cat to fend off loneliness, but an English friend offered her one, which, the friend suggested, she might secrete in her room; she would have to tip the maid with some silence money, but the cat was well-behaved—a box in the bathroom with some newspapers would do. So, she brought the cat to her room, under her coat, and had it for company during the winter. But presently the cat died. So she had to dispose of it. She made up a neat little bundle and was about to put it into the incinerator when the proprietress greeted her. "This will never do," she said to herself, and went off to the library. On the way, she passed a likely-looking place to ditch the cat, a culvert or something, but this time a bobby came around the corner just in time to deter her—she thought he might ask questions. On her way to lunch, the guard called to her to tell her that she'd forgotten her parcel. "This is getting to be funny," she said to herself. But she resolved on taking a bus ride and leaving the cat on it. But as she rose to leave, a passenger tipped his hat and handed her her forgotten parcel. She tried to leave it at the restaurant where she ate lunch. But here the waitress prevented her. And again she was foiled on a subway ride. Just about desperate, she phoned the friend who had given her the cat. "Bring it out," the friend said, "and we'll take it to the pet cemetery in the neighborhood." So she did. When she got there, she thought she'd take one last look at her beloved cat and opened the parcel. It was a leg of mutton!

Current oral versions of "The Dead Cat in the Package" tend to drop the apartment-dweller's-dilemma theme, substituting the idea that a cat was accidentally run over by a car, and the body was retrieved by the remorseful driver. The theft —directly from the car—takes place at a shopping center rather than a downtown store, but then everything lately is moving to the suburbs. Also, at least in the Salt Lake City versions I have heard, the actual stealing of the cat package is witnessed by the car owner, which allows for a new ending. Both of the following texts are set in a popular Salt Lake City suburban mall.

Linda relates this true story about a friend and her mother who tried to finish some last minute Christmas shopping. While they were hurrying out to the Cottonwood Mall, facing the holiday traffic, a cat found itself under the tires. The mother, who was driving, felt terrible as she saw its poor form on the cold road. She decided that the cat deserved more than to be left in the street to be battered by the unfeeling traffic. She carefully placed the cat in an empty plastic prestigious Castleton's bag and laid it on the back seat, intending to bury the cat upon arriving home. They resumed their journey and were fortunate to find a parking space. Before reaching the entrance, they instinctively looked back, only to discover a lady walking straight toward their car. Curious, they watched while the lady snatched the Castleton's bag and scurried to her car. They quickly returned to their car to follow the thief. Their travels led them to a K-Mart store. The lady, tired from running, had stopped at the snack bar to order a drink. Her prized package was still nestled in her arms. They watched as her fingers gently slid into the bag to discover its secret contents. She fainted in horror, not to be revived by the efforts of the store personnel. An ambulance was called. The last time they saw the lady she was being carried away on a stretcher, her precious package across her stomach.

The last-minute Christmas shopping is a nice touch in this story, since it accounts for both the accidental killing of the cat in heavy traffic as well as for the thief prowling the parking lot looking for valuable packages left in unlocked cars. In other local versions the thief is revived, but she faints again immediately when she sees the cat package on her stomach.

The second Salt Lake City version is attributed to Mormon

ward "Home Teachers," congregational tutors in Latter-day Saint religious doctrine, an important localized detail undoubtedly added to enhance the believability of the story. The supposed location of the cat killing—near a school—is significant because it furnishes a valid reason for picking up the body. The attribution of the story to a human source at least three storytellers removed from first person is, of course, typical of urban legends:

> The ward Home Teachers told us of an incident which they said had occurred to a friend of Brother Alan Phipps' mother-in-law. He [Brother Phipps] said that the friend had been driving near a school when she hit a cat on the road and killed it. Not wanting the children coming home to see the dead cat lying in the road, she put it in a plastic bag and threw it behind the seat as she was parked in the road. The friend then proceeded to drive to the Cottonwood Mall where she got out of her car and walked toward the entrance. She was shocked to see another woman open the door of the car she had just left and take the bag containing the cat. The same unknown person then got in her own car and drove to the other side of the Mall. The friend followed in her own car, incensed that someone would rummage through her automobile. The unknown woman entered the Mall at the southeast entrance and turned into the small Penney's restaurant there. The friend continued to watch her. She then opened the plastic bag, shrieked and fainted. The waitress got the hostess who called for an ambulance as the patrons of the restaurant gathered around the still-unconscious woman. The rescue squad arrived and put her on the stretcher. Someone, a patron or a waitress or somebody, noticed the plastic bag she had carried into the restaurant and carefully placed it on the stretcher at her side.

The most remarkable version of "The Dead Cat in the Package" I have seen came to me by sheer coincidence all the way from the East Coast from Dan Arnow a student who took my American Folklore class in 1973 at the University of Utah. His source was a local woman, Dorothy R. Goode, described by Arnow in his paper as "a very alert, spry, and with-it seventy-five year old lady" born in New Jersey. She remembered being told the story there by her father when she was about eight years old. I reprint it—"The Ham Cat"—exactly as Mrs. Goode typed it, with her permission:

In the winter of 1906 when I was a small girl, our family lived in a little town in New Jersey. Each work-day my father boarded the Erie local commuter train to go to his office in New York City. The ride took almost an hour. My father and three friends occupied the time playing cards. Two of the men got on the train at a town up the line and secured two seats so that when my father arrived they could turn over the back of one of the seats and when the fourth member arrived they could all sit facing each other, spread out a newspaper for a table and enjoy their game. The fourth member got on at the next stop. On a Monday morning this man arrived with a large brown paper package. Upon being questioned he told them that their old family cat had died over the week end and since the ground was frozen hard he wasn't able to dig a hole to bury it. So his wife suggested that when he was on the ferry boat from Jersey to New York, that he just toss old pussy cat overboard.

The cat had died curled up and since rigor mortis had set in, was solid and somewhat frozen. The wife wrapped him carefully in brown paper and tied the package securely.

On reaching Jersey City the four friends hurriedly boarded the ferry and were engrossed in discussing the game and since it was bitter cold they stayed in the cabin. In about ten minutes they were at the end of the ferry trip and the man still had the cat. Nothing to do but take it to his office and do the job on the return trip that evening. He put the cat on the fire escape to keep cool.

The four friends met again at the ferry terminal, got on the boat, discussed the day's events and in no time they were on the other side again. With the cat. The train was crowded and they were unable to sit together. The man with the cat put his package in the rack and enjoyed his newspaper until passengers alighted at the next stop and again the four could sit together, turn over the back of the seat and resume the game of the morning. The man with the cat hardly heard the conductor call out his stop, rushed to the exit, remembered his package, ran back and grabbed the package over the seat they were occupying and got off the train just in time.

On reaching his home his wife scolded him when she saw he still had the package. She took it from him to put it out on the back porch when she noticed the package was a little different. Upon opening it she found a nice 14-pound ham! The poor man didn't join his friends for three weeks. He rode in another car. The person who got the cat might recognize him!

This version belongs to Subtype B in which a more desirable package is accidentally substituted for the corpse. But it is dated almost fifty years before anyone reported the story again, and it has been enlarged upon with wonderfully elaborate details of people and places. The mode of transportation is a ferryboat rather than a bus or car, and the characters are all men. Everything is so true-to-life that you almost expect to be given the score in the card game, right along with the exact weight of the "nice" ham. Evidently the legend is much older than the folklorists' few texts had heretofore suggested.

Let us return to Herb Caen's second San Francisco cat story, which is probably related to "The Dead Cat in the Package." It also involves a cat which is accidentally run over, but the pet is now assumed to have been the victim of food poisoning:

> . . . a family goes mushroom hunting, and, upon returning home, begins worrying about toadstools. So they feed a mushroom to their cat—that's nice—and since the beloved pet survives, they begin eating mushrooms at a great rate. Suddenly, somebody looks out the window,

and there's the cat on the lawn, stone cold dead. Exeunt all to Central Emergency for a stomach-pumping. When they get home, the milkman (garbageman, laundryman) has left a note. He ran over the cat by accident, and he's sorry.

This legend condemns the California family for testing the uncertain food on their "beloved pet." The way *I* heard it ("The Poisoned Pussycat at the Party") the family was having a grand dinner party with a large baked salmon as the main course. Just before the guests arrive the cat is caught in the act of nibbling a piece of the fish, so the hostess kicks him out the back door and arranges a lemon slice and some parsley over the bite marks. Later that evening the cat is found dead on the back porch, and all the dinner guests must be told the awful truth and taken to a hospital to have their stomachs pumped. It spoils the party, but even worse is that the next-door neighbor admits to the hostess the following morning that she ran over the cat in her driveway the night before and placed the corpse quietly on the back porch so as not to disturb the party guests with the sad news.

Perhaps related to all this is a news story that appeared during a recent New York City garbage strike. One man is supposed to have disposed of his garbage (a "dreadful contamination"?) every day by wrapping it nicely and leaving it on the seat of his unlocked car. Invariably someone stole it.

"The Runaway Grandmother"

"The Runaway Grandmother" is another popular urban legend in which a corpse is unwittingly pilfered from a car. The death-in-the-family theme implicit in "The Dead Cat in the Package" (the pet as a quasi-relative), is made explicit here: an actual human relation of the family dies. Disposing of her is the problem, not only as a practical and legal matter, but also because death confuses and upsets people. When an unlucky stranger solves the problem, the family feels relief and release from the tension of confronting the graphic reminder of their own mortality.

Both the dead cat and stolen grandmother stories focus on the bereaved and tend to create in their climaxes a feeling of uneasiness tinged with humor. It is this emotional tone, shared by the legend audience, that links the stories, not any necessary historical connection. The legend of "The Runaway Grandmother" has its own characteristic motifs. While the cat legend usually begins with the problem of corpse-disposal, in "The Runaway Grandmother" this problem occurs unexpectedly in the course of the story, and the motivation for hiding the body is entirely different. There is never an exchange of goods motif in the grandmother heist.

An American folklorist, Robert H. Woodward, noted some of the similarities between the two stories in a 1963 news article in the San Jose, California, *Mercury;* he characterized the grandmother's corpse legend as "an addition to the growing store of urban tales," and he paraphrased it as follows:

> A local resident reports as fact an experience of a Washington State family that he knows. After the family had crossed the Mexican border on a vacation trip, one of the children said, "Mama, Grandma won't wake up." Upon discovering that Grandma had died, the family placed her body in a sleeping bag and secured her to the top of their automobile, planning to report her death to the police at the first town. While they were in the station, their car was stolen—with Grandma's body still aboard. No trace has yet been found of either Grandma or the car. Another resident reports the tale as having happened in Italy.

It should also be noted here that, in common with the London version of "The Dead Cat in the Package," this story involves Americans who are abroad when their funerary problem comes up. Part of their distress seems to come from not being on home ground.

The first text of "The Runaway Grandmother" legend published in a folklore study was also collected in 1963, from an English woman who heard it told in Canada by her cousin who in turn had heard it in Leeds. (Obviously the story was getting around pretty well by 1963.) The characters in this version—and several of their terms—are definitely English. Parallel to the Americans visiting Mexico, these tourists have their odd experience during a vacation in Spain:

> This story was told me by my cousin, who had heard it from a friend in Leeds, about a couple whom he knew, who went for a camping holiday in Spain with their car. They had taken his stepmother with them. She slept in a different tent to the others. On the morning that they struck [broke camp], they were very busy, and they didn't hear anything of her for a while, and then, when they went to her tent, they found she had died, and rigor had already set in. They were in a great state, and they didn't know what to do, but they decided to roll her up in the tent, and put her on top of the car, and go to the nearest town, and go to the consul and the police. So they did this, and went to the town, and then they felt very cold and miserable, and they hadn't had a proper breakfast. So they thought they'd get a cup of coffee to revive them, before they went in search of the consul. So they parked the car, and went to a small cafe, and had their cup of coffee, and then came back to look for the car. But it wasn't there. It had gone.
>
> So they went home to England without the car or the stepmother. But the difficulty was, they couldn't prove [i.e., probate] her will.

Since "The Runaway Grandmother" probably entered American folklore from European tradition, it is not surprising that some American versions have their setting in a simple unspecified "Europe." The following well-detailed text was collected in 1966 from an Indiana student who had "heard it from her mother as a true event." Unlike the English tourists in Spain who stop to eat out of sheer hunger, misery, and exhaustion, the Americans in this tale pause more for standard touristic reasons, in order "to . . . eat their last European meal at a small, quaint restaurant." The loss of their grandmother seems to strike the family as almost comical:

> Well, once there was this family and they had been waiting to go abroad for, oh, a number of years, and finally their big chance came. They packed up all of their things—had their car shipped over—and were soon in Europe and ready to go sightseeing. There were five of them and they had a rather small car and it was pretty crowded. There were the two parents and two children and a grandmother.
>
> Well, a trip to Europe can be quite a strain on an old woman. And she hadn't been in too good of health anyway, and that was one of the reasons they took the trip, so she could see all of the "European Wonders" before she died.
>
> Anyway, one day when they woke up they found that the grandmother had died during the night. Well, they didn't know what to do because here they were, 3,000 miles away from home and across an ocean yet, and they were the grandmother's only living relatives so they couldn't just send a body back to the States with no one to receive it. They were going to be starting home soon, anyway, so out of desperation they wrapped the grandmother's body in a piece of canvas and tied it on the top of their small car—which, by the way, made much more room inside the car.
>
> And as they were making their last round across the village where they were staying they decided to stop and eat their last European meal at a small, quaint restaurant.
>
> Well, it happened that while they were in there someone stole the car with the grandmother on top. For some reason they weren't too worried about the whole situation, they just wondered what the looks on the crooks' face would be when they discovered the strange contents of the canvas.

THE VANISHING HITCHHIKER

English folklorist Stewart Sanderson found "The Runaway Grandmother" second in popularity in Great Britain among "motor-car stories" only to "The Vanishing Hitchhiker." His collection of versions of the legend extended back to more than twenty years before the earliest American texts. Sanderson wrote:

> I first heard it in Leeds in 1960, from the wife of a colleague who told it as having happened to friends of her friends in Brussels, as they escaped through northern France during the German invasion of 1940. A few weeks later, believing with my informant that the tale was true, I repeated it to an academic colleague in Edinburgh who also knew her. To our initial surprise he had recently heard much the same story from a colleague in Cambridge, with the difference that it was set in Spain after the war and involved the difficulty of cremating the corpse. . . . Other variants involve the loss of a body in a caravan [trailer] which slips its tow on a hill; the theft of a body from the luggage compartment of a holiday-tour bus; and a variant I collected at the University of Nsukka, Nigeria in 1965. In this, the body of an old woman, being taken back for burial at her native village on the Crow River, is lost by rolling off the roof of a mammy-wagon [local bus] into the bush.

The European versions, then, seem to fall into two distinct subtypes—one, the wartime story involving crossing an international border, usually to escape the Nazis or to leave Eastern Europe; and second, the postwar tale of vacationers abroad. Indiana folklorist Linda Dégh, who assembled more than one hundred versions of "The Runaway Grandmother" and related stories from Europe and the United States, believed that the legend must have acquired its common form during or just after the Second World War. Possibly it evolved from stories known in Europe in the eighteenth and nineteenth centuries dealing with the mistaken theft of a corpse and ending with the thieves' shock as they inspect their booty. In the wartime context, Dégh speculated this story could have lost its last episode, shifting the climax to the risky crossing of an international border. In later years, and especially in American tradition, the focus seems to have shifted again to emphasize the inconvenience and distress of disposing of a corpse while on a vacation in a foreign country. The "message" of the story, Dégh suggested, derives from "the fear of the return of the dead" and expresses the concern that "the corpse has to receive a decent burial." In addition to the United States and England, Dégh encountered "The Runaway Grandmother" both orally and in print in Norway, Sweden, Denmark, Germany, Switzerland, Italy, Poland, Hungary and Yugoslavia. The completion of her comparative study of all texts ought to clarify further the legend's history and development.

Folklorist Charles Clay Doyle was more willing than Dégh to connect "The Runaway Grandmother" to earlier narratives. He pointed to a Renaissance "jest" (a very grim joke, at best) widely known in Europe in which an Italian Jew attempts to send his dead Jewish friend back home to Venice illegally by pickling the dismembered corpse in spices and honey and packing the pieces in a jar. While he is on a boat during the trip home, various parts of the corpse are stolen and eaten by an unwary Florentine. The switching of corpse and food, Doyle suggested, may link this story also to "The Dead Cat in the Package" (cat swapped for meat). The motif of gnawing or nibbling on a corpse is of course also found in a number of other terror stories similar to "The Roommate's Death." If one agrees that all these tale plots *are* linked, then it would seem that the bereaved family is not just ready to abandon Grandmother, they are willing to devour her as well, or at least they toy with the idea.

Two details in texts I have collected might lend support to Doyle's analysis. First, Doyle's Renaissance jest is strangely similar in one respect to the 1906 version of "The Dead Cat in the Package" ("The Ham Cat") which took place partly on a ferryboat; and, second, I have heard versions of the dying-grandmother story in which the corpse is cremated abroad and sent home to relatives by mail. The recipients later say "Thanks for the good curry powder; we've been using it on everything."

Whether the American versions sprang directly from postwar European variants of the border-crossing tradition or not, the particular subtypes found here are distinct. Of eighteen American versions which Dégh collected in Indiana, for example, ten fall into the group represented by the first text given above, in which the family is traveling in Mexico when the grandmother dies. The second largest group (five texts), in which the vacation takes place in the Western desert, is evidently influenced by an incident in John Steinbeck's *The Grapes of Wrath* (1939): Granma Joad's corpse being taken through the California agricultural inspection station wrapped in a blanket on the back of a truck. (Of course, it is possible that Steinbeck deliberately introduced legendary material into his plot.) Here is a summarized version of the desert subtype told to a student by a Gary, Indiana, woman who "was almost in a state of shock," believing the story to be true:

> It happened to her friend's family (I don't know their names) as they were traveling across the desert to California. Within this station wagon there was a father, a mother and their children, and the mother-in-law who everybody called "Grandma." And as they were going across the desert Grandma became sick and she died. Now they didn't want to alarm the children and they didn't want to leave Grandma out in the desert so the only place they had room for her where she—her smell wouldn't bother the children—was to strap her on top of the station wagon along with the baggage with a tarp over her, of course. And as they were traveling across the desert they kept looking for a town where they could deposit Grandma. They finally arrived in a small town in Arizona where they stopped at a filling station and they went in to report Grandma's death. And while they were within the

filling station somebody stole the station wagon and when they went out—no station wagon and no Grandma! Well, it wasn't very funny even though it sounds like it because they have to wait seven years now to prove that Grandma is dead before they can collect any insurance. And they've never been able to find either the car or Grandma. This actually happened.

In a third American subtype—or it may be just Midwestern —the family is vacationing in the upper Peninsula of Michigan when Grandma dies. In a text quoted by Dégh, the stripped car is found some weeks later, but Grandma's corpse never turns up.

One cannot help being struck by the American versions' casual—almost callous—treatment of the old woman's death. Often the initially crowded condition of the family car is mentioned, and the decision to make more room by putting the corpse on the roof is made by the survivors without hesitation or debate. There is almost always a reference to the practical difficulty of probating the will or supplying proof of death. Yet almost never is any significant mention made of the car, baggage, and other property also lost to the thieves; it is almost as if this was the price the family had to pay for the relief of being rid of Grandma.

Alan Dundes has analyzed various versions of the legend and concluded that its central message is the rejection of old age and dying in our youth-oriented society. It is significant, he felt, that there is "much more room inside the car" when Grandma is gone—the old lady is out of the way at last. But yet "Grandmother is a burden whether alive or dead"—her body is an unwelcome reminder of human mortality and it must be kept away from the children. Furthermore, although the family "took her for a ride" (and Dundes recalled how gangsters use that phrase), an anonymous third party (the thief)—like a mortician in real life—took care of her after death. Finally, Dundes interpreted the details at the end of the legend as suggesting that Americans' principal interest in their aged relatives is the prospect of inheriting their money. Both the frequent news articles and editorials about the treatment of aged Americans and examples of the "Theater of the Absurd" provide validation of this critique of American values. For the latter, compare how the same themes are handled in two of Edward Albee's most gripping plays, *The Sandbox* and *The American Dream*.

"The Runaway Grandmother" is a fully-developed modern legend widely circulated today in many different versions across the United States; still, each story, with its often elaborate local details, is told as a "true" account. There are recent examples of each of the subtypes (the wartime and the postwar). The following was told by a Tucson, Arizona, man to my student Ann Clegg in Fall 1969. It was supposed to have happened to a friend of the informant's, "a prominent businessman in Tucson." Here the family travels to Mexico, and the thieves, usually not identified in the story, are said to be native-American "foreigners":

> The businessman went on a trip to Mexico with his wife and his grandmother. The grandmother had always wanted to go to Mexico, and as she was quite old, they knew this would probably be her last chance to go. ["Taking her for a ride" again?]
>
> They got somewhere in the remote mountain areas and the grandmother had a heart attack and died. The odor was terrible because of the heat and because the grandmother had a bowel movement as she was dying. (Apparently this is not uncommon when a person has a heart attack. [Student's comment])
>
> They wrapped the grandmother in a piece of canvas they had to cover their suitcases with and put her body on top of the car. They stopped in the first town with a telephone—a town populated mostly by Indians. It took quite a while to contact their relatives in Arizona and

when they came out, the body had been stolen! Imagine how frightened those superstitious Indians must have been when they found they had stolen a body!

Ah yes, this is how the superstitious savages will react to a corpse, at least in the American folk stereotype. But why would they steal a car in the first place, and how could they conceal the vehicle? We "real Americans," the story shows, know better how to regard death—rationally and neatly.

A second Utah report of "The Runaway Grandmother" indicates that the earlier form of the story is still circulating. Early in 1979 I found this note on my desk left by my assistant Sharon Decker Pratt who had often heard me discuss this and other urban legends:

> Last night at a dinner party our friends told of a conversation they had just had at a dinner party Friday night with a fascinating woman originally from Latvia who is staying at Snowbird [a ski resort] this week with some mutual friends. (The hostess was also originally from Latvia.) Both women were recounting various experiences they'd had during various political regimes; the horrors, the resistance movement, and even some of the more humorous things.
>
> The guest is around fifty, either a doctor or a dentist (kept referring to her patients) in Boston, and a perfectly reliable, credible-sounding individual. Anyhow, she told of her family's departure during the '40's whereupon her grandmother died just as they were to leave the country. Inasmuch as it was very cold (zero in the middle of winter) the grandmother's body was frozen solid and, since they did not want to leave her body in Latvia but rather bury her elsewhere, they decided to wrap her as a rather long piece of luggage and take her with them out of the country, along with their other belongings.
>
> Well, you guessed it!!! Someone stole the grandmother at the train station.

THE VANISHING HITCHHIKER

This is all very well, except that Mrs. Pratt telephoned me on Monday to say that she had spoken to the woman again, and it was the grandmother of *another* Latvian friend whose corpse had been stolen.

NOTES

"The Dead Cat in the Package"

Dorson's *American Folklore* was published by the University of Chicago Press in 1959; its last chapter contains several references to other well-known urban legends, with "The Dead Cat in the Package" discussed on pages 253 to 254. The Herb Caen column quoted in this chapter was published in the *San Francisco Chronicle* on 25 August 1963. Someone ought to do a study of all the urban legends Caen has printed, and usually debunked, over the years.

Albert Howard Carter included five urban legends in "Some Folk Tales of the Big City," *Arkansas Folklore,* 4 (August 15, 1953), 4–6; the two dead cat stories set in Washington, D.C., and London quoted in this chapter appear on pages 5 to 6. University of Utah student Harriet Welsh turned in the two suburban Utah versions quoted in Fall 1975, and the story continues to be popular in Utah oral tradition.

"The Runaway Grandmother"

Robert H. Woodward reported the item in the San Jose *Mercury* in his note "The Stolen Grandma," *Northwest Folklore,* 1 (1965), 20. The 1963 English version (travelling via Canada) was published as tale number 48, "The Stolen Corpse," in Katherine M. Briggs and Ruth L. Tongue, ed., *Folktales of England* (Chicago: University of Chicago Press, 1965), pp. 99–100. Stewart Sanderson discussed English and other European versions of this legend in "The Folklore of the Motor-car," *Folklore,* 80 (1969), on pages 251–252.

The two quoted Indiana texts, plus information about Linda Dégh's collection and her planned study come from Dégh's note in *Indiana Folklore,* 1 (1968), 68–77, titled "The Runaway Grandmother." Further discussion of Dégh's material is in the article by her and Andrew Vázsonyi, "The Memorate and the

Proto-Memorate," *Journal of American Folklore,* 87 (1974), 229–230. Charles Clay Doyle published his article "Roaming Cannibals and Vanishing Corpses" in *Indiana Folklore,* 11 (1978), 133–139.

Alan Dundes' interpretation was part of his essay "On the Psychology of Legend," in *American Folk Legend: A Symposium,* Wayland D. Hand, ed. (Berkeley and Los Angeles: University of California Press, 1971), 21–36; he discussed "The Runaway Grandmother" on pages 33 to 36.

6 Dalliance, Nudity, and Nightmares

Many urban legends, as we have seen, have the same basic features as classic ghost stories or tales of terror: apparitions, hidden menaces, assaults and murders, contamination, and the presence of the dead. However, another important group of legends is not sinister in the slightest; as in farce or contemporary situation comedy, the worst threat to the protagonist is the humiliation of having his intended infidelity or naked body publicly exposed.

At least the hint of illicit amorous adventure is present in most of these urban legends. Sometimes the situation is clearly one of dalliance, and getting caught in the act—or at least caught *preparing* for the act. So realistic are the plots and so ordinary the characters that it seems completely possible not only that such nightmarish adventures could have happened, but also that they could happen again to anyone.

I was taken in by one of these stories myself when I was a relative beginner in folklore research.

"The Solid Cement Cadillac"

One day in the early summer of 1961 shortly after I had received my Ph.D. in folklore, I lounged on a beach along Lake

Michigan with family and friends and daydreamed about my first teaching job beginning in the fall at the University of Idaho. As it happened, a neighbor of my parents there in South Haven, Michigan, began to tell us about a funny incident that a cement-truck driver in a nearby town had experienced recently, and her story soon had my full attention. Her family's own local business was ready-mix cement, but this story involved a driver for a similar company in Kalamazoo.

It seems that he was delivering a load of wet mix to an address near his own neighborhood when he decided to detour slightly and say hello to his wife (or perhaps it was to pick up something at home). When he came in sight of his home, he saw a shiny new Cadillac in the driveway, and he parked the ready-mix truck and walked around the house to investigate. He heard voices coming from the kitchen, and when he looked in through the window there was his wife talking to a strange, well-dressed man. Without checking any further, and certainly without alerting the couple inside, the truck driver lowered a window of the new Cadillac, and emptied the entire load of cement inside it, filling the car completely. But when he got off work that evening and returned home, his tearful wife informed him that the new (now solid-cement) car was for him—bought with her hard-earned savings—and that the stranger was the local Cadillac dealer who had just delivered the car and was arranging the papers on it with her.

I made a mental note of the story, for even though it seemed to have some corroborating details (police had been called, a wrecking company towed the car away, the actual weight of the cement was given, the effect on the car described, name of the cement company provided, possible news stories on the event recalled, etc.), it had the ring of other urban legends I had heard and studied. I was not prepared to say at once that it was "only a legend," but I did wonder how a noisy ready-mix truck could have parked—let alone unloaded—directly outside a house with two people chatting quietly inside without their noticing. It also seemed strange that no one had clipped the news story, perhaps to post it in the local family's cement business office as a warning to their own drivers.

Late that same summer in Moscow, Idaho, I received in the mail volume I, number 1 of the *Oregon Folklore Bulletin* and read this notice which accompanied a request for further versions:

> An interesting story is presently circulating in all parts of the United States. It is told as if it were right out of last week's newspaper, and concerns a cement-truck driver who stops by his own house for a mid-morning cup of coffee while on the way to deliver a load. But when he drives down his street he notices that there is a flashy car parked in front of his house, and . . ."

The significant variation in the story was that the driver "finds his wife and a strange man in a compromising situation and sees that he is a bit too late to intervene successfully." Hence, instead of a merely ironic tone, the story implies criticism of the wife's behavior and in part shows her punishment.

In the next two issues of the *Oregon Folklore Bulletin* the editor, Barre Toelken, reported on his findings about the story. In Fall 1961 he described "a plethora of versions mailed from all over the country," and in the third issue of the *Bulletin* (Winter, 1962) he gave a summary of the forty-three versions then on file. Most had been sent in from the Northwestern states, but Utah, Illinois, and Massachusetts were also represented, along with my version from Michigan. The majority of the accounts contained authenticating details about police, tow trucks, or newspaper reports, but no verifiable proof. While such details—the make and model of the car, for example—varied, only two other versions had significantly different plots: in Utah, the car belonged to the company boss who had come to make arrangements for a surprise party in recognition of the driver's faithful service to the company; in Massachusetts, the car was said to be one that the wife had just won in a raffle.

THE VANISHING HITCHHIKER

Another Idaho folklorist, Louie W. Attebery of the College of Idaho in Caldwell, succeeded in tracing a documented "original" of the story. He introduced the account of his findings, published in 1970, as follows:

> Quite likely every folklorist has encountered versions of the urban tale of the cement truck dumping its contents into an empty car. . . . When I first heard folklorists discussing this cement-truck tale, I waited for a lull in conversation. (I was new then in this field and didn't know that lulls don't come often.) I wanted to suggest that this was an example of the connection between history and folklore, for I *knew* that a cement truck had unloaded its contents into a car in Denver. I was living there at the time.

Attebery's check in the morgue of the Denver *Post* produced three news stories of August 5, 6, and 7, 1960, concerning one Robert O. Porter, driver of a truck for the Centennial Concrete Co., Denver, "who dumped five tons of concrete mix into a pal's car," after he tried to deliver an order of wet mix and was kept waiting for an hour. The car, owned by his "pal" Joseph Nelson was a 1946 DeSoto, and when the cement settled down in it, the *Post* reported, "its tires blew, its springs snapped and its frame bit the dust." Although some details of the case, such as the age and relatively low value of the car and the publicity gained by the company (which replaced both the car and the cement) strongly suggest that the incident was an advertising gimmick, the car itself, according to Attebery, "sits in a place easily seen from one of Denver's arterial streets and serves as a pop advertisement for the cement company." The final proof that this "Solid Cement" DeSoto is not after all the original of the urban legend was the discovery of the existence of an *earlier* version.

In a response to Attebery's request for information on the story, Professor Américo Paredes of the University of Texas, Austin, reported that at the 1960 annual meeting of the

Texas Folklore Society in San Antonio April 15 and 16, 1960 —four months before the Denver incident—"a discussion period following the reading of a paper generated the recital of the load-of-concrete episode." In the meantime, the Denver story had reached Texas; Paredes was able to send Attebery an Associated Press news story and wirephoto about the Denver incident (August 6, 1960, from the Fort Worth *Star-Telegram*) in which the weight of the doomed DeSoto had climbed to six tons. So it appears that oral tradition and journalism each contributed to the growth of this legend, both elaborating on the details of the basic plot.

Probably because of the relative lack of variation in "The Solid Cement Cadillac," as well as the need to expend considerable time and energy to search newspaper files or police records for earlier reports, American folklorists have not paid further attention to the story other than to keep on recording it from their students and acquaintances. This tale, like "The Death Car," tends to run in cycles of popularity. Most versions mention a specific local car dealer, cement company, or auto-wrecking yard, but it has never been possible to establish any of these businesses as the real origin of the legend. Clearly, the continued popularity of the story in the United States is as a satisfying example of an unfaithful or unjustifiably suspicious spouse—for once—getting what he or she deserves. However, the legend also contains a warning that the avenger ought to be absolutely sure of the evidence before doing something drastic. Thus, the truck driver, who looks like a decisive hero at first, is shown up at the end as an impulsive fool victimized by his completely false assumption. Another likely appeal of the story is that it shows a blue-collar truck driver trying to get back at a rich man and his fancy car.

The important role of the press in circulating and varying legends has been nicely shown by Norwegian folklorist Reimund Kvideland, who made a study of European newspaper reports of the cement-filled car story which began to appear in the spring of 1973. The first story he found was in a short news item (which I have translated below) in the Bergen, Norway, paper *Bergens Arbeiderblad* (March 6, 1973):

TERRIBLE REVENGE OF A LOVER

A Bergen citizen who several days a week drives a ready-mix cement truck as a second job the other day came by his own residence and saw a friend's car with a sun roof parked there. He stopped the cement truck and went in the apartment building to say hello. But sounds from the bedroom gave him to understand that it wasn't him but rather his wife that the fellow had come to visit. Without disturbing the couple in the bedroom, the man went back out of the building and over to his friend's car. He pulled the sun roof back and backed the cement truck alongside it. Then he switched on the delivery system and filled the parked car with about two cubic meters of cement. When the lover came for his car, the cement was completely hard.

Later in the evening the car was towed away. The case has not been reported to the police.

Despite the brevity of the published story, several familiar details are present—sounds from the apartment, a specific amount of cement, the tow truck, and the police. It belongs to the subtype in which the wife is really guilty. (Indeed, all the European versions insisted on the wife's guilt; never does the car turn out to belong to the truck driver after all.)

On the day after the article appeared, Kvideland reported, many Norwegian newspapers got the story from news bureau wire services or reporters and published variations on it. The national paper *Dagbladet,* for instance, ran a highly detailed story identifying the driver as a twenty-six year old man, pinpointing the car as a 1966 Volkswagen, and painting a lurid image of the lovers being spied "naked in a double bed."

The solid cement Volkswagen weighed 2.6 tons and required a couple of tow trucks to move it away. The lover, *Dagbladet* concluded, after consulting with an insurance company, decided to ask the police to investigate the matter.

In the next few days essentially the same story was published in the Copenhagen *Politiken,* the Stockholm *Aftonbladet,* the London *Sunday Mirror,* and, on March 12, in the Nairobi, Kenya, *Daily Nation,* under the headline "Concrete Revenge." Meanwhile, back in Bergen, the reaction from a rival local newspaper had already called the truth of the original account into question.

On March 9—three days after the appearance of the story in the *Bergens Arbeiderblad*—the Bergen newspaper *Morgenavisen* ran a page-one teaser that "Today's Little Tidbit," the solid cement Volkswagen story, was fully explained on page seven. There the tale was unmasked as nothing but a traveling legend (*vandresagn*), as well known in West Germany and Denmark as in Norway. The facts were, the paper proudly revealed, that no Bergen tow-truck company had pulled in a cement-filled car, no insurance company had a record of the case, the police knew nothing about it, two cubic meters of cement would weigh closer to five tons than two and six-tenths, a Volkswagen couldn't hold that much anyway, and even if it could, the windows would have popped out and a single tow truck could have handled the weight.

Bergens Arbeiderblad was forced to admit that the story was indeed only an "international journalistic-joke." In an article accompanied by a cartoon showing the cement being poured through the sunroof, the editors traced the wanderings of the story, "probably from Germany or Denmark" to Bergen, and thence to "half the world." The paper's original source had been a cement-truck driver who had not explained to the reporter clearly enough that he was relating not a recent incident but a story he had heard some three years before. The *Arbeiderblad*'s mistake was not immediately forgotten; Kvideland's study includes a photograph of a cement-filled Volkswagen beetle taking part in the Bergen 17th of May (Norwegian Independence Day) parade of 1973!

Given the even earlier appearances of the story in American sources (evidently unknown to the Norwegian journalists), Kvideland concluded that the origin of the legend was certainly to be found in the United States. The difference between the appearance of a Cadillac or other large expensive car in the legend here and a tiny sunroofed Volkswagen bug in Norway is an apt commentary on different lifestyles and economic conditions. Also, it removed the possibility of the getting-even-with-the-wealthy message for the story in Europe.

"The Nude in the RV"

It was really quite simple, an American tourist explained to Royal Canadian Mounted Police who found him wandering along a highway near here clad in his undershorts. His story:

His wife was driving the family car, while he relaxed in a trailer. She stopped to let some bears cross the road and the husband stepped out to see what the trouble was.

His wife drove on.

The police drove 70 miles before overhauling the wife and reuniting the couple.

The Associated Press news wire carried this amusing little story datelined Prince Albert, Saskatchewan, on August 3, 1962, and doubtless many newspapers picked it up. The *Salt Lake Tribune*, for instance, ran it on page one the next day under the headline "Bare Hiker—Bear Alibi." The Canadianism, "overhauling," in the last sentence gives it a convincing air of genuine local color.

This legend should perhaps be called "The Nude Out of his RV [Recreational Vehicle]" or "The Lightly Clad Fellow Left Behind." The uncovered man—and it is always a man—is not simply napping in the nude, or nearly so, while riding in his

camper or trailer; instead he finds himself abruptly thrown
out of it—"into the streets of Pleasantville," as one folklorist
put it.

"The Nude in the RV" shares several themes with other
legends. As in "The Runaway Grandmother," the American
tourists suffer an inconvenience while abroad and on the road.
As in "The Solid Cement Cadillac," intervention of the police
is mentioned to help validate the story. And, of course, like so
many modern legends, an automobile is central to the plot. It
should come as no surprise then, given these traditional elements, that the story is not a true account, despite the newspaper publication of it.

The best evidence for the news report's traditional character
is that we can trace an earlier version many hundred miles
east. "Bert and I" (Robert Bryan and Marshall Dodge), the
Maine dialect raconteurs, recorded a variant of the story a year
earlier, in 1961; they recounted the story of how Harry Whit-
field startled Wiscasset, Maine. Harry's wife, Margaret, was driving their truck camper, and Harry was inside just stepping
into his pajamas when a sudden jerk of the vehicle propelled
him out into the street. He took refuge in a phone booth, for-
getting that it was glass-sided and had a light that would go on
when he closed the door. In his striped PJ's he was mistaken
for an escaped convict. When it was all finally straightened out,
Harry cautioned his wife, "Next time, Maggie, let the clutch
out slow." The record album notes claimed that the story was
"inspired by a true anecdote of a man who really did tumble
out of his camper naked onto the main street of Wiscasset."

Professor Edward D. Ives of the University of Maine at
Orono confirmed for me that this is indeed a popular oral story
in Maine, not a "true one," of course, although "practically
everyone who has heard it was told it as an actual happening."
As he wrote:

> I have heard many versions of that story. . . . scarcely
> a year goes by that I don't hear a new one. The classic

133

version as I get it is not of a camper but a trailer. He's exhausted and wants to go back and lie down (which is illegal in moving trailers). Tells wife to say nothing if cops stop her, or rather to say that she's alone and no one is back there.

The Maine oral versions of the legend conclude in the usual way, according to Ives.

Other folklorists have found the incident reported as really happening in a number of other states. In Maryland it occurred "at a crossroads, in the midst of nowhere;" in the Midwest a dentist from Brazil (the Indiana town of that name) was returning from a long exhausting camping trip out west when misfortune struck just a few miles away from home. Professor Ronald L. Baker of Indiana State University, Terre Haute, received a wonderfully-detailed oral text of this particular variation from a student in 1967:

A VACATION

A couple of years ago, this dentist in Brazil thought it was about time he and his wife took a vacation. They had both worked pretty hard, and he decided that they really needed a vacation. He thought if they were going to make a trip out west he might as well do it right. He went out and bought a brand new camping trailer and a new car to pull it. The trailer wasn't just one of these fold-out deals. It was a big furnished trailer.

Well, they went to Colorado, and stayed two full weeks and really had a wonderful time. The only thing hampering their good time was that the husband had done all of the driving, and was really pretty tired. He didn't think his wife was a good enough driver to drive on strange land. Especially with all the new equipment he had bought. He had tried to be very careful, and nothing had gone wrong. Things were going very smooth.

Well, they got all the way to Marshall, Illinois, when

they stopped to get something to eat. The man was just exhausted from doing all the driving. They were trying to drive straight through without stopping over night. They spent so much time on the way out there, they wanted to make up for it coming back. As I said before though, the man was very cautious not to get a speeding ticket. Anyway, after they stopped in Marshall to eat, the man decided to let his wife drive the rest of the way home. He was so exhausted he could hardly keep his eyes open. It was only about thirty-five miles to their house, and she was familiar with the highway, so he felt pretty confident about letting her drive the rest of the way. He even decided to crawl back in the trailer and lay down. So he undressed down to his boxer shorts, and must have just went to sleep.

When the woman had driven all the way to Fruitridge and Wabash [in Brazil], she had to come to a stop for the red light. Well, her husband felt the car stop, and opened the back of the trailer to see where they were at. Just as he opened the door, the light changed and the woman pulled off. The trailer gave a little jerk and the man fell out. There he was in the intersection with just his shorts on. Well, he ran into the Clark gas station there on the corner. Incidentally, his wife didn't know he had fallen out, and kept on driving. Meantime, the man gets this gas station attendant to drive him home in a truck. They passed his wife on the highway, but she didn't even see them. The man tells the driver how to take a short cut, so, they beat his wife home. She still doesn't know he's not in the back, and she gets caught in a traffic jam in Brazil. Meantime, the truck driver drops the guy off at home. He didn't have a key to get in, so he gets a lawn chair out of the garage and lays down on it. They live in the country, and he wasn't too worried about anyone seeing him in his undies, so he just sat the chair in the driveway. Well, he dozed off, and just about that time his wife pulled in the driveway safe and sound. Half way up the driveway, she sees her husband sitting in the chair. Well, it scared her so bad that she stepped on the gas instead of the brake and ran the whole damn thing right through the garage.

The more elaborate conclusion of this version which brings the man home instead of leaving him dangling, so to speak, has become the preferred ending lately. I have heard it this way in oral tradition reported from New York and New Jersey, and it is this form which appeared as the preface of Dan and Inez Morris's how-to book *The Weekend Camper*, published in 1973. The Morris account, which took three full pages, was presented as "A True Story" with only the names allegedly changed from the presumed incident to "protect the unfortunate couple." The tourists' vehicle is a pickup truck camper, their itinerary includes Canada and Mexico as well as the United States (shades of "The Runaway Grandmother" and the 1962 Associated Press story!), and the wife stops while deciding which fork of a road to follow. At the end of the story the husband, clad only in undershorts, is watering the lawn—hoping his outfit will pass for a bathing suit—when his wife comes home. She drives straight through the rear wall of the garage. The authors offered a three-point rationale for beginning the camping book with the story, and drew lessons from it along the following lines: "Have rear-vision mirrors on both sides of recreational vehicles. And use them constantly. Know what's going on behind you as well as in front of you."

"The Cut-Out Pullman"

Although "The Nude in the RV" did not blossom until the early 1960s when privately owned vacation campers and trailers were becoming commonplace, it has a clear prototype in a legend that was familiar to American railroad workers and passengers at least twenty years earlier. Folklorist Wayland D. Hand published this version of the older story in 1971:

A New York businessman was once returning home
from a conference on an overnight New York Central
train. Since he was fagged out and couldn't sleep, he
went to the club car for a nightcap at about ten or eleven
o'clock, clad only in a silk bathrobe and house slippers.
An unattached woman of considerable charm was at the
bar, and they soon fell into conversation. After a few
drinks the businessman announced that he had to turn in
because of a big conference in New York the following
day. The girl suggested that he might care to find one
for the road in her compartment. Against his better judg-
ment he accepted. What went on is glossed over, but can
be inferred from the fact that he woke up next morning
in the Pullman yards in Buffalo, bereft of his wallet. The
girl, who probably had pulled this trick on many an un-
suspecting customer, had failed to tell him that she was
in the Buffalo car.

The train went on to New York, where the man's wife
and children were there to meet him. When he did not
alight, the children kept asking, "Where's Daddy?" The
wife asked George, the porter. He replied, "He has to be
somewhere close by, Madame, for his clothes are still in
the berth."

A day or two later, with the help of Travellers' Aid,
the man returned to New York and sheepishly confessed
to his escapade with the girl who victimized him, leaving
him stranded in a strange city, without either money or
clothes.

Many ticket agents, porters, brakemen, and other railroad
workers told Hand that they knew variations of this tale, including several involving only the shoes of passengers being
rerouted after they had been collected by a porter for overnight shining. One might speculate that as railroad travel de-
clined following World War II, the gist of the story—male
passenger stranded nearly nude—was transferred to other vacation vehicles; conversely, if the energy crunch forces Americans

back to the trains in large numbers, it is possible that, "The Cut-Out Pullman" may revive at the expense of "The Nude in the RV."

Nudes and More Nudes

Nudity surprised is too good a joke—and too common a nightmare—not to be a recurrent theme in contemporary story-lore. For example, Linda Dégh heard the following rumor in Budapest in 1960, which seems to be related to "The Nude in the RV" legend, about a bachelor living in a highrise apartment who had just turned his bath water on and undressed one evening when the newspaper was delivered to his front door. Stepping out in the hallway to bring it in, stark naked, he became trapped outside when his door blew shut and locked. Dégh suspected that this was merely a literary plot retold orally and traced it to *Twelve Chairs,* a novel by the Russian satirists Il'ia Il'f and Evgenii Petrov published in 1928. I have heard a similar story in the United States, but it may have been inspired by the 1970 Mel Brooks film based on the novel.

Another variation of the bare-body theme is "The Disintegrating Bathing Suit." The most recent version I have seen appeared in the *Manchester Guardian* in 1979. The newspaper reported that an American writer in the south of France invented a story he cabled back to his newspaper about "a millionaire's party with the usual international guest list, but distinguished by culminating in an early morning bathe in gift-wrapped swimsuits cunningly designed to disintegrate on contact with sea water." Whoever originally thought up the story, it has been told for years, either with a suit that falls apart or one that becomes transparent in salt water (since it was only tested inland, and this flaw in the material went undetected).

Not quite nude, but clearly embarrassed for his lack of complete cover, is the young man or rumor and legend who finds himself seated at a dinner party with his fly unzipped. Often his future in-laws are the hosts (as in some versions of "The Nude Surprise Party," below in this chapter); his fiancée kindly whispers a warning. In Subtype A of "The Unzipped Fly" he tries to distract the dinner guests' attention by suddenly pointing out the window—"Hey, look at that!" His embarrassment is only compounded, however, since two dogs are copulating on the front lawn just at the same moment. In Subtype B he slyly zips before getting up from the table, except that he snags the tablecloth into his fly zipper and pulls all the dishes to the floor when he arises. It is amazing how many newly-engaged young men have reportedly suffered such chagrin and shame from the same cause. All of these nude and partially-dressed stories undoubtedly get their bite from their distinct plausibility and likelihood—flies do come unzipped, or are left unzipped, after all, though not always at dinner parties.

One recent caught-in-the-nude story deserves special attention because the victim, for once, is a woman.

In late 1975 a correspondent asked advice columnist Ann Landers which letter in twenty years' time had caused the greatest reaction from her readers. Ann said it was one about a housewife who liked to do her housework in the nude. Among the thousands of responses to this, largely from women who confessed to the same preference, was a summary of a "news item [unidentified] about the Ohio housewife who was doing her laundry in the basement" when . . .

> She impulsively decided to take off her soiled housedress and put it in the machine.
>
> Her hair was in rollers and the pipes overhead were leaking. She spotted her son's football helmet and put it on her head. There she was, stark naked (except for the football helmet), when she heard a cough. The woman turned around and found herself staring into the face of the meter reader. As he headed for the door his only comment was, "I hope your team wins, Lady."

Some oral versions of this story provide better reasons for the situation: the dress is put into the machine because there are not enough clothes for a full load, and the surprised intruder is the plumber who had been called by the husband to fix those leaking pipes. Five years later Ann Landers was still referring to this as her most notorious column, but the text she printed early in 1980 had undergone several verbal alterations.

The plots and punch lines of these legends vary, but the appeal of a story of a hapless man or woman in a state of undress apparently never flags. It is a theme as old as Lady Godiva or Adam and Eve.

"The Nude Surprise Party"

The theme of nudity surprisingly revealed continues to fascinate, as Freudian dream analysis would lead us to expect. In first-person versions of another legend on this topic we even seem to hear the voice of a neurotic patient speaking to an analyst and describing an anticipated party that becomes a nightmare. The plausible plot involves either a businessman who lusts for his beautiful secretary or a young couple who yield to sexual temptations.

In her column for June 28, 1976, Ann Landers printed this well-told gem, "The Nude Surprise Party," credited to an otherwise unidentified newspaper called the *Shining Mountain Sentinel* which had been sent in as a "humdinger" by a reader signing himself "Ann Fan":

> I woke up early feeling a little depressed because it was my birthday and I thought, "another year older," but decided to make the best of it. So I showered and shaved, knowing when I went down to breakfast my wife would greet me with a big kiss and say happy birthday, dear.
>
> All smiles I went into breakfast and there sat my wife reading the newspaper as usual. She didn't say one word.

So I got myself a cup of coffee and thought to myself, oh well, she just forgot. The kids will be in in a few minutes all cheery and they will sing Happy Birthday and have a nice gift for me.

There I sat, enjoying my coffee, and I waited. Finally the kids came running in yelling, give me a slice of toast! I'm late! And where is my coat? I'm going to miss the bus!" Feeling more depressed than ever I left for the office.

When I walked into the office my secretary greeted me with a nice smile and a "Happy birthday, Boss" and said, "I'll get you some coffee." Her remembering made me feel a lot better.

Later in the morning my secretary knocked on my office door and said since it's your birthday why don't we have lunch together. Thinking it would make me feel better I said that's a good idea.

So we locked up the office and since it was my birthday I said why don't we drive out of town and have lunch in the country instead of going to the usual place. So we drove out of town and went to a little out-of-the-way place and had a couple of martinis and a nice lunch, and started driving back to town when my secretary said why don't we go by my place and I will fix you another martini.

It sounded like a good idea since we didn't have anything to do in the office anyway. So we went to her apartment and she fixed us both a martini and after a while she said if you will excuse me I think I will slip into something more comfortable and she left the room. In six minutes she opened her bedroom door and came out carrying a big birthday cake and following her was my wife and all my kids and there I sat with nothing on but my socks.

Several features of this spicy tale, besides the highly suspicious too-neat plot, suggest that it belongs to modern folk tradition. The punctuation, especially of quotations, is erratic; the verbal tag "so" appears frequently; and the repetition of

"there I sat," echoed by "there sat my wife," indicates the pol-
ish of a repeated story. In fact, various forms of this legend
have had both oral and written circulation in the United States
for more than fifty years.

The first-person version, sometimes titled "The 49th Birthday" and almost always concluding "nothing on but my socks,"
is typical of its appearances in current "Xerox-lore," a category
of folklore that circulates in the form of copy-machine dupli-
cates of typed or handwritten accounts. A third-person version
of the legend usually begins "The boss of a medium-sized office
had hired a steno who was out of this world"; it generally ends
with the office staff gathered in the stenographer's bedroom
singing "Happy Birthday" to their naked boss. This one may be
titled simply "Surprise!" These two stories have passed widely
from hand to hand in duplicated copies since at least the mid
1960s, and the "Surprise!" version was printed a decade earlier
in a book called *More Over Sexteen* (1953). One popular but
quite different Xerox-lore variation describes the philandering
businessman (in this case successful with his secretary) who
tries to stimulate his weary sex organ manually the same night
during the intervals when his pretty and eager wife is out of
the room preparing drinks, fixing dinner, and donning her sexy
nightgown. Then, finally, she springs her *big* surprise: "Honey,
we're on Candid Camera!"

Professor William Hugh Jansen of the University of Kentucky published and compared twenty-eight versions of the
"Nude Surprise Party" tale, calling it "The Surpriser Surprised"; he commented that the hapless businessman in some
way conspired in his own embarrassment because he "under-
estimated his wife's memory, overestimated his secretary's pli-
ability, and overestimated his own sexual appeal." He is,
Jansen concluded, "a high class schnook or a noodle." Jansen's
only American oral version of the story which involves an
imagined liaison between office acquaintances was told to him
by a Kentuckian who had heard it in 1962 as a joke:

In this version the setting was an office, the two main characters being a female secretary and a new male accountant.

The secretary was a single, very attractive young woman and the man promptly asked her out. She refused him many times and he became more and more determined to win her favor and take her out.

Finally, after many weeks of consistent efforts, the secretary approached the man and invited him to her apartment for dinner. All through the meal she hinted at a surprise for him. Instantly drawing his own conclusions, the man became very excited.

After dinner she excused herself and stated that she was going to prepare for the surprise. Completely mistaking her true meaning for one of a sexual nature, the man removes all his clothes and when she asks him if he is ready, he immediately answers yes and she flings the door open, revealing the entire office staff, gathered to celebrate his birthday. (Jansen, A-9)

This form of the story seems to have international circulation, for Jansen received another example of it that a professional colleague in Newfoundland had heard in Wales during the middle or late 1950s. It concluded: "With one jump he opens the door and rushes in, stark naked. His wife, children, secretary and all his staff are standing there with a big sign saying: 'Happy Birthday to You.'" (Jansen, A-12)

In American oral tradition "The Nude Surprise Party" is more commonly told as a legend ("true") rather than a joke (fictional). The characters (as well as most narrators) tend to be younger people; often they are an engaged couple, or are celebrating an anniversary, usually the young woman's birthday. Both the man and the woman become victims of the surprise. Jansen himself first heard this form of the story in Massachusetts (but told about New Jersey) in 1935. The earliest known text, however, was one that another Kentucky teacher had written down in a local mountain dialect in 1927: a married woman decides to entertain a "foreign" man (a traveler from outside the mountains) when she is left alone at home on her birthday. The story concluded (local names and terms are explained in brackets):

Now, old Sibo [the husband] had heared of these here quare women [eccentric women] on Troublesome [a creek; the region where they live] a-givin' surprise birthday parties, so he'd got one up for his woman, asking in all her neighbors and her Pap and Mom and other relates [relatives]; and just as Sile [the wife] come into the front room naket [naked] from the kitchen house [cooking shed out back on the property] and the ferriner [the outsider] leaped to his feet and run to meet her, Sibo and the company come in the front door a-hollerin' "Surprise! Surprise!" (Jansen, A-13)

A more typical example of the surpriser-surprised tradition, also from Jansen's study, is this modern oral version collected in 1959, thirty-two years after the preceding story; it was supposed to have happened in Somerset, Kentucky:

There was a young couple of well-to-do families who were engaged to be married. On the girl's birthday, the two of them went out, but returned home rather early. Upon returning to the girl's home it was discovered that the parents were away. The two of them decided to do something "different" and removed all their clothing. Soon thereafter, the telephone rang. When she answered it, the girl was asked by her mother to please go to the basement and turn off the automatic washer, which she had forgotten. When the conversation ended, one of the couple decided it would be fun if the boy carried the girl downstairs piggyback. This they proceeded to do, and when they reached the bottom of the stairs, the lights came on and a large group of friends and relatives yelled, "Surprise!" The girl, I was told, had a nervous breakdown

and was institutionalized. The boy has neither been seen
nor heard of since. (Jansen, A-3)

Professor Jansen's versions came primarily from the Midwest,
because that is where he collected folklore most consistently,
but similar stories are known much more widely. The instiga-
tor of the sexual activity may be either the male or the female
partner, but the outcome is normally more tragic for the girl
(she goes mad and is locked up) than for her boyfriend (he
leaves town). Sometimes the boy has just returned from college
or from military service when the surprise party occurs; in other
versions he escapes into the services after being surprised. The
specifics of the denouement vary, but a descent downstairs
(which Jansen interpreted as a Freudian symbol) and the frequent appearance of a minister in the party group are fairly
consistent details.

The piggyback ride is a common motif in more recent versions of the tale. These invariably describe a couple who are
baby-sitting together when they are summoned below by a
request to do some household errand such as turning on a
washer or clothes dryer. (The effect is something like that in
"The Nude Housewife" story in which the woman's nudity
is revealed in the laundry room.) The ruined celebration is normally in honor of their forthcoming marriage rather than a
birthday party. This representative text was collected in 1961:

A young girl, who was engaged to be married, was
asked to baby-sit with her young cousin. She agreed to do
so, and invited her fiance to sit with her. During the
course of the evening they became passionately inclined,
took off their clothes, and frolicked about the house. While
giggling and pushing one another around, the boy heaved
the girl on his back in piggyback style and bounced her
through the rooms. Going past the door to the basement,
they heard a sound, and the boy teasingly said he was
going to take her down in the basement with the spooks.
He gropingly took her down the stairs in the dark. When

they reached the bottom, a light came on and the girl's parents, the minister, and many prominent people of the community jumped out from their hiding places and yelled, "Surprise!" They had arranged a surprise bridal shower for the couple. The boy dropped the girl from his back, ran up the stairs, grabbed his clothes, and fled from the city. It was later learned that he had joined the Navy, and never again contacted the girl. The girl lost her mind, and was committed to an asylum. (Jansen, C-5)

The confrontation in the finale between the parents, the minister, and "prominent people," on the one hand, and the passionate couple on the other, is obviously symbolic of the irreconcilable clash between middle-aged upholders of traditional values and young people who no longer accept the old morality. Strangely enough, even though the story is told mostly by young people presumably sympathetic to the couple, the consistent lesson is that the old morality triumphs—in these stories much more savagely than in the boss-secretary tales.

Jansen also collected two versions told from the disapproving adults' point of view: in one the previous sexual experience of the couple is hinted at (so it serves them right to be caught!), and in the second the surprise party is actually a trap set for the couple by friends of the people for whom they are baby-sitting, to see if the young people are really fooling around (they are, of course). Jansen was certainly correct in calling this last one "a malicious little narrative" which "leaves a bad taste in the mouth."

Still More Nudes

The ministerial presence in several versions of "The Nude Surprise Party" perhaps links them to other traditional plots involving men of the cloth themselves innocently caught out of their clothes. Jansen heard this evidently transitional legend in 1970:

There was this Baptist couple who were real important people in the church. It was the woman's birthday and her husband had planned a surprise party for her. While she was upstairs taking her shower that night, the minister and the rest of the church people were led in by the husband and hidden behind chairs in the living room. His wife, upon finishing her shower, walked down the stairs and stood naked at the bottom and hollered to her husband, "Come and get it while it's clean!" (Jansen, A-15)

In a somewhat similar folk story the husband, unknown to his wife, brings the minister home for dinner after helping him with some yardwork at the church, and invites him to use the shower upstairs to clean up. The wife, all unawares, comes upstairs, hears the shower, and reaches in through the curtain to grasp the bather's penis; she tugs it several times saying "Ding, dong, dinner bell!" Then she faints when she meets her husband emerging from the downstairs bathroom. Also comparable to these is a story popular among Utah Mormons. Two Relief Society teachers (female) visit a young Latter-day Saint woman whose husband happens to be taking a shower at the time. Unaware of the guests, he struts out wrapped only in a towel, flips the cover aside as he passes the doorway of the room they are in, and sings out, "Did you ever see a dream walking?"

Still recognizable as belonging to the same narrative family, but minus a minister, is this story submitted by a University of Utah student in 1969:

The lady came home from the grocery store, and she saw her husband working under the car. All that was exposed were his legs, so in passing she reached down, unzipped his zipper, chuckled to herself, and went into the house. Immediately she saw her husband sitting in the easy chair reading a newspaper. She cried, "Who is THAT under the car?" and her husband replied, "My mechanic." She told her husband what she'd done, and they went outside to find the mechanic lying unconscious, in a pool of blood, because when the lady unzipped his pants he was so startled he sat up and clobbered his head under the car.

"The Fart in the Dark"

In an important group of "Surpriser Surprised" legends the central character is humiliated, not by nudity exposed, but by a "Fart in the Dark"; Jansen called them the "flatulent form" of the surprise party tale. In brief, a victim of stomach gas is either left in a darkened room or blindfolded and assumes incorrectly that he or she is alone. Then the person relieves himself or herself of the gas by breaking wind. This story, like the nudity ones, has had considerable underground circulation as Xerox-lore, often with a title like "The Gastronomical Bean Story," in which an unfortunate bean gourmet has imprudently feasted on his favorite food. Carson McCullers included the story of the blindfolded farter in a room full of people gathered to celebrate his birthday in *The Heart is a Lonely Hunter* (1940). Recent oral versions have moved the scene of the shame to a car, the favorite location for urban legends popular among students, as, for example, in this 1976 Utah text:

> A plain Jane girl in school, who has never been out on a date, no boy friend, etc. One day the captain of the football team asks her to go to a big dance. She runs home overwhelmed—has her hair done, new dress, nails manicured, and prompts her parents on how to act. In the process of getting ready the chili she had for lunch starts making itself known. Near 7 o'clock (the time he'll be there) the gas is getting unbearable. She feels about to bust. Just before she can get relieved, the doorbell rings. She lets him in, introduces him, but by this time she can hardly talk and is breathy. So she begins plotting how to get rid of it before she blows it. So, she plans that when he opens the door to let her in, she blows on his way

around the car, rolls the window down, fans it out and everything will be fine. He opens the door for her, closes it, and starts to walk around. She lets it out, and it sounds like a howitzer, the windows vibrate, the license falls off, etc. She rolls the window down, fans it out, and is all cool and composed when he gets in. He smiles and says, "Oh, I'd like you to meet Ruth and Bob" who are sitting in the backseat.

Like all of the "Supriser Surprised" legends this story holds all the terror of a bad dream from which one cannot immediately wake up. What makes it worse is that such mistakes and misunderstandings do occur in everyday life, not only in nightmares. Someone may actually plan a surprise party for us at any time, and stomach gas cannot be denied forever. The stories warn against jumping to easy conclusions, but it would still be *so* simple to do so if we were presented with a similar set of circumstances. In common with the obviously fictional *jokes* about sex and scatology, these legends provoke a laugh at loaded topics; the difference, however, is the possibility of a real-life occurrence of such embarrassment, and the oral performance style which presents these as true stories.

NOTES

"The Solid Cement Cadillac"

Barre Toelken, editor of the *Oregon Folklore Bulletin,* published his query and follow-up information on "The Solid Cement Cadillac" in Vol. I, No. 1 (1961), pp. 5–6; No. 2 (1961), p. 3; and No. 3 (1962), pp. 2–3. Unfortunately, this modest mimeographed newsletter died at that point before Toelken was able to publish all the variants he had received, although he alluded to the story again in his essay "The Folklore of Academe," which is Appendix B in Jan Harold Brunvand, *The Study of American Folklore,* 2nd. edn. (New York: Norton, 1978), p. 376.

Louie W. Attebery's note titled "It Was a Desoto," appeared in the *Journal of American Folklore,* 83 (1970), 452–457. He quoted the full texts of both the longest *Oregon Folklore Bulletin* report on the legend and all three of the Denver *Post* articles.

THE VANISHING HITCHHIKER

Reimund Kvideland's study "Det stod i avisa! Når vandrehistorier blir avismeldingar" was sent out as a 1973 Christmas greeting from the University of Bergen Institute of Folkloristics and Regional Ethnology. The title means "It was in the newspaper! When Traveling Legends become Newspaper Copy." Translations from his study are my own.

A clipping about the supposed 1973 event in Bergen, Norway, from the Swedish paper *Aftonbladet* (March 8, 1973) was sent to Louie Attebery by Ingemar Liman of Stockholm and then kindly forwarded to me by Attebery.

"The Nude in the RV"

Barre Toelken published an example of the August 3, 1962, Associated Press story on "The Nude in the RV" from an unidentified northwestern newspaper in *Oregon Folklore Bulletin*, 2:1 (Winter-Spring, 1963), 5. He also alluded to the story in his essay "The Folklore of Academe," in Jan Harold Brunvand, *The Study of American Folklore,* 2nd edn. (New York: Norton, 1978), p. 376, from which I quote here. I located my copy of the news story in the *Salt Lake Tribune*.

The Maine version was recorded on *The Return of Bert and I* by Robert Bryan and Marshall Dodge (Ipswich, Mass.: Bert and I, Inc., 1961); see side two and the liner note. The information from Professor Edward D. Ives was in a personal letter to me dated February 8, 1979.

George G. Carey summarized the Maryland tradition of this legend in *Maryland Folk Legends and Folk Songs* (Cambridge, Maryland: Tidewater Publishers, 1971), p. 81. The version in *The Weekend Camper* (Indianapolis and New York: Bobbs-Merrill, 1973), pp. ix–xii, was mentioned by Ronald L. Baker in his article "The Influence of Mass Culture on Modern Legends," *Southern Folklore Quarterly*, 40 (1976), 373; Professor Baker kindly sent me a copy of the actual published text as well as the oral version from Indiana quoted in this chapter. That story was collected by Baker's student Delana Good from Ruth Haverty in December 1967. Also, as Baker pointed out, a variation of "The Nude in the RV" story appeared in the Doris Day and Brian Keith film (1968) "With Six You Get Eggroll."

'The Cut-Out Pullman" and More Nudes

Wayland D. Hand's article "Migratory Legend of 'The Cut-Out Pullman'; Saga of American Railroading," appeared in *New York*

Dalliance, Nudity, and Nightmares

Folklore Quarterly, 27 (1971), 231–235, with the quoted text on pp. 231–232. Linda Dégh and Andrew Vázsonyi report the nude-bachelor-locked-out rumor in their article "The Crack on the Red Goblet or Truth and Modern Legend," published in *Folklore in the Modern World*, Richard M. Dorson, ed. (The Hague: Mouton, 1978), pp. 253–272. "The Disintegrating Bathing Suit," a story I have heard at least since the early 1960s, is mentioned in an article by Harry Whewell titled "Crunch Questions" in the *Manchester Guardian* (September 9, 1979), p. 19.

I have versions of "The Unzipped Fly" from Salt Lake City back to 1967, but it is surely an older story and it is definitely still current. The Ann Landers column quoted containing the nude housewife story was published on December 7, 1975. The next column I spotted it in appeared on February 3, 1980. In Erma Bombeck's version of the same story the housewife is wearing her son's full football uniform when the washer repairman arrives; he comments, "I hope your team wins, lady." See *Aunt Erma's Cope Book* (New York: McGraw-Hill, 1979), pp. 11–12.

"The Nude Surprise Party"

William Hugh Jansen's study "The Surpriser Surprised: A Modern Legend" appeared in *Folklore Forum*, 6 (1973), 1–24; I have used the reprint in Jan Harold Brunvand, ed., *Readings in American Folklore* (New York: Norton, 1979), pp. 64–90. The index numbers of Jansen's texts are given after each quoted example in this chapter. Professor Jansen's analysis and all twenty-eight versions provided in his study are well worth consulting. He suggested a number of new folk motif designations appropriate for the legend cycle, such as Q495.4* *Naked appearance before friends as punishment for dalliance.*

Alan Dundes and Carl Pagter's *Urban Folklore From the Paperwork Empire*, American Folklore Society Memoir Series, vol. 62 (Austin, Texas, 1975) contained two examples from this tradition circulated as Xerox-lore. "Surprise!" is on pp. 97–98, and a text of "The Fart in the Dark" (victim blindfolded) appears on pp. 98–99. Other examples were published in Cathy M. Orr and Michael J. Preston, ed. *Urban Folklore from Colorado: Typescript Broadsides* (Ann Arbor, Mich.: Xerox University Microfilms, 1976), pp. 148–150 ("The Gastronomical Bean Story," "The Bored Business Executive," and "The 49th Birthday").

More Over Sexteen, edited by J. M. Elgart, was published in New York by Grayson Publishing Corp. in 1953; a version of "Surprise!" is on p. 50.

THE VANISHING HITCHHIKER

G. Legman reported "The Stranger in the Shower" story (pulling the penis), told as true, in 1940 in his monumental study of sex jokes *Rationale of the Dirty Joke* (New York: Grove Press, 1968), p. 710. Marianne Faulkner collected "The Unzipped Mechanic" story for a class of mine during Fall quarter, 1969.

"The Fart in the Dark" was given brief treatment in McCullers' *The Heart is a Lonely Hunter* (Bantam Books edn., 1970), p. 202. An anonymous student contributed the 1976 Utah version of the legend.

7 | Business Ripoffs: Two Favorite Media Legends

Mass media

The mass media, as we have seen, are not unconducive to the survival of urban legends. On the contrary, print or broadcast references to current legends—whether seeking to validate or debunk them—almost always serve to spread the stories farther. Often the media stories supply new details and add to the confusion. The folk themselves participate in this process when they mail such stories as "The Hook" or "The Nude Surprise Party" to newspaper columnists or call them in to radio talk shows.

Folklore in general has not withered in our mass communications society, and some urban legends in particular have flourished with the help of widespread news coverage. The more these tales are written about, the more they are talked about, and vice versa. As the careers of the two following urban legends demonstrate, the unverified oral report of a supposed published news story may itself become an element of folklore, so that statements like "I read this somewhere in a newspaper," (which may often be true) are now as much verbal formulas as "Once upon a time" or " 'Twas in the merry month of May" were formerly in traditional folklore.

The pair of urban legends which best illustrate the interaction of news media with oral tradition exploit the popular distrust of business establishments; in the first example the villain is a famous hotel, in the second, a local department store.

"Red Velvet Cake"

Traditions about restaurant foods are not always as stomach-turning as "The Kentucky Fried Rat." In this story, the red velvet cake is tempting and delectable; it is the institution which serves the cake that is the nasty element in the plot. The story is frequently told in the first person, although the tale is just as doubtful as any other urban legend. Detailed recipes for the cake exist, but only in written or printed form. The following typical account collected in 1973 from an Oregon informant referred to a supposed experience of a close friend in California:

> Our friend, Dean Blair, got on a bus in San Jose one morning and shortly after, a lady got on the bus and started passing out these 3×5 cards with the recipe for "Red Velvet Cake." She said she had recently been in New York and had dinner at the Waldorf Astoria and had this cake. After she returned to San Jose, she wrote the hotel asking for the name of the chef who had originated the cake, and if she could have the recipe. Subsequently she received the recipe in the mail along with a bill for something like $350.00 from the chef. She took the matter to her attorney, and he advised her that she would have to pay it because she had not inquired beforehand if there would be a charge for the service, and if so, how much it would be. Consequently, she apparently thought this would be a good way to get even with the chef.

The recipe:

> Cream together:
> ½ C. shortening
> 1½ C. sugar
> 2 eggs

Make paste of 2 T. cocoa and 2 oz. red food coloring. Beat well, add to creamed mixture.

Add 1 tsp. salt and 1 tsp. vanilla, to 1 C. buttermilk (Do not make your buttermilk). Add alternatively with 2½ C. sifted cake flour to creamed mixture. Beat and beat. Mix 1½ tsp. soda and 1 T. vinegar; fold into mixture. DO NOT BEAT. Bake in two 9-inch pans 30 min. at 350°.

The frosting: 5 T. flour, 1 C. milk cook until thick, stir constantly. Let cool. Cream together 1 C. sugar, 1 C. butter or margarine, 1 tsp. vanilla. Add to flour mixture. Beat until consistency to spread. Looks like whipped cream.

Although the special recipe with a high price in folklore is occasionally for a super candy ("The Million Dollar Fudge"), "Red Velvet Cake" featured at the Waldorf Astoria is the more standard element in this legend. Probably this hotel/food combination gains some credence from two other hotel-food names, Parkerhouse Rolls (named for a Chicago hotel) and Waldorf Salad. There are countless variations on the lady's hometown, the amount she paid for the recipe, and the lawyer's explanation for why she must pay the bill. Getting the information by mail (or COD) is not the most usual way—generally the recipe is sent to the diner from the kitchen—but the revenge motif is characteristic. Often the offended lady gets even with the chef by including the recipe in her Christmas card, serving it to her bridge club with a mimeographed or oral explanation, or sending it to a local newspaper for publication. In fact, newspaper reports of the story, complete with the full recipe, are the best evidence we have for the widespread knowledge of the "Red Velvet Cake."

The recipe from the Oregon source is fairly standard. There are signs of typical folk style and variation in the admonition "Do not make your buttermilk" and the instructions "Beat and beat." The order and the amounts of ingredients vary only slightly from version to version, with even the firm command in capital letters "DO NOT BEAT" appearing repeatedly. A light creamy white frosting nearly always accompanies the cake recipe, and the information that when finished it resembles whipped cream is also traditional. Actually, the cake is not at all bad—if you like red cake—and I have enjoyed it several times in my folklore classes when students have felt that they could convince me by serving the ACTUAL CAKE(!) that their own mother (aunt, grandma, neighbor lady, etc.), always a woman, was the true original victim of the Waldorf's greedy chef. There's no doubt about it; the cake can be made, and it frequently has been, but the Waldorf is in no way responsible for creating it.

My own earliest exposure to the "Red Velvet Cake" legend dates from 1961. It is a stained and tattered mimeographed sheet that a Home Economics teacher at the University of Idaho distributed to her class. A student who in 1965 heard me discuss the story dug the sheet out from old class notes that had been kept by one of her sorority sisters. The Home Ec teacher—who said she learned the legend from a friend who in turn had heard it in a restaurant "some years ago"—headed the handout sheet "RED VELVET CAKE AND ITS STORY"; in this version the victim was a woman from Seattle who had been dunned $300 for the recipe. The story's conclusion is "Since the price of the recipe had been costly to her, she decided all her friends should enjoy baking and eating this luscious and extravagent [sic] RED VELVET CAKE." The teacher then added her own comment that "The 2 oz. of food coloring is the correct amount, and this is the reason for the color and texture of red velvet."

There seems to be a strong tradition of the "Red Velvet Cake" story in the northwest, not only in Idaho, Washington, and Oregon, as already illustrated, but also in Canada. The January 1962 issue of the Canadian-Pacific Railroad magazine *Spanner* referred to it as "much publicized lately" and attributed it to "a B.C. [British Columbia] woman" who was obliged to pay $200 for the recipe. No specific hotel was named. "Dorothy Dean's Homemakers Service" of the Spokane, Washington, *Spokesman-Review* included a recipe for "Red Velvet Cake" in May 1962, as part of a handout of favorite recipes. There is no mention of a hotel here, but the instructions for making the cake are traditional—"do not beat," "consistency of whipped cream," and so forth. By late that same year the concept of a bright red cake seems to have been strongly established, judging from a Wrigley's Gum advertisement I clipped from the December, 1962, issue of *Woman's Day*. It pictured a bright red cake with thick white frosting as a "Holiday Cake" and gave directions for preparing it from a packaged white cake mix and one-half ounce of red food coloring. The cake is promoted as a Christmas treat and "a gay idea for New Year's too."

Two other 1960 clippings in my file show further distribution and variation on the story. The *Jackson* [Mississippi] *Daily News* for Thursday, December 19, 1963, published a red cake recipe that was standard in every way except that apple cider vinegar was one of the ingredients. The contributor of the recipe was quoted: "This Red Velvet Cake recipe is one that came to me from a friend in Yazoo City. . . . I understand it originally came from the Waldorf Astoria." The *Phoenix* [Arizona] *Gazette* for January 23, 1964, headlined a story "$300 Recipe Shared." The steep price, in this case, was paid only for the *frosting* recipe. The article explained:

> The title is fitting because, as one Phoenician (who prefers to remain anonymous) tells us, it comes from a woman who wrote a famous hotel in New York asking for their delicious cake frosting.
>
> The hotel obliged and also enclosed a 300 dollar bill for their "services." Needless to say she was shocked but trips to her lawyer proved to no avail; she had written for a favor and they had "sold" it to her.
>
> Now her only satisfaction is to publicize her $300 purchase. Here it is . . . and cheaply at that . . .

(I have also encountered a generalized "$400 [chocolate] Cake" recipe and a story which mentions only "a lady in a restaurant" as the source.)

Wondering if there were any truth to the recurring story, I wrote the Waldorf Astoria hotel inquiring about this famous cake in 1965. The prompt response was quite a surprise: it included details that showed the legend was even more widely known and varied than I had suspected. The hotel public relations director revealed that:

> . . . we have letters and clippings in our files going back more than ten years which give numerous versions of this story. The cake is sometimes described as a chocolate cake and other times as a red velvet cake and the price varies from $5 to $1,000. A thorough check was made here at the hotel when the story cropped up initially and it is completely false.

The letter concluded with the information that the hotel policy was to supply free of charge any recipes from their menu either to hotel guests or food editors who request them, but that the executive chef could not recall ever using such a recipe as "Red Velvet (or Red Chocolate) Cake."

Unfortunately, I did not have the sense at the time to request a look at the Waldorf Astoria's letters and clippings; when I did ask to do so fourteen years later, I was informed that "We do not keep a clipping file because the clippings are too numerous to store."

A few examples from Salt Lake City, Utah, are representative of the media material that continues to fuel the legend. The *Salt Lake Tribune* food editor gets frequent requests for the recipe and on occasion she publishes it. In the April 13, 1975, issue of the *Tribune* a recipe was published for "Waldorf Red Velvet Cake" with "Waldorf Frosting." Again, in 1979, the request appeared on the foods page, and about three dozen readers—all different from the earlier group—sent in their recipes. The food editor, in publishing one of them on

August 23, 1979, commented that the cake had "received recognition world-wide and should be included in your list of favorites to try."

The reply letters which I saw in 1979 suggested that there is now a tradition of the cake and its recipe even apart from the Waldorf story. Only one reader actually submitted the hotel legend (which had not been asked for), commenting that her sister told it to her as the "$100-Cake" story. However, several other readers referred to the cake either as "Waldorf-Astoria Cake" or "The Famous Waldorf Astoria Christmas Cake." A number of readers mentioned the Christmas angle, and one said her family also liked to have the red cake on Valentine's Day and Independence Day. All of the recipes called for mixing the red food coloring with the cocoa to form a paste which is then added to the creamed "wet" ingredients. One reader commented, "Fussy to make, but good and pretty."

Surely there are hundreds of other media mentions of "Red Velvet Cake" and probably thousands of folk accounts, both oral and in the form of recipe cards and notes. I suspect that some American somewhere eats "Red Velvet Cake" and hears the story dozens of times each week, especially during the Christmas season. A "complete" collection of variants would be almost impossible to compile, but it would be a fascinating job to undertake. However, a final irony is that lately life has begun to imitate folklore; that is, the Waldorf Astoria now distributes a "Red Velvet Cake" recipe to those who inquire.

A story datelined New York in *The Denver Post* (December 20, 1978) caught my eye; it was an interview by reporter Rose Dosti with executive chef Arno Schmidt of the Waldorf Astoria hotel. Schmidt stressed the importance of low-calorie natural foods on his current menus, and he "refused to share his recipe for red velvet cake requested by many readers." He insisted in the interview, "Forget the red velvet cake and take my white chocolate mousse."

But *"his* recipe for red velvet cake"; how could that be?

Once more I wrote to the hotel, and I was answered that the legend was still absolutely "untrue." But this time (1979) the chef (unnamed in the letter) claimed to remember the cake:

> [he] says that the recipe goes back many years, and it has never been a particularly delicious cake, or a favorite. Also, it does not reflect contemporary taste and standards because of the use of artificial coloring.

Enclosed with this reply was a duplicated copy of directions for making "AUTHENTIC WALDORF RED VELVET CAKE," and the recipe was completely standard except for the lack of any chocolate or cocoa. (The omission was explained in a note: "Apparently there are some recipes around that include cocoa, and the recipe has been called 'Red Velvet Chocolate Cake.'") Also, the *icing* for this "authentic" Waldorf recipe included the strictly non-traditional addition of "red food coloring to suit."

Personally, I don't think that this attempt by some chef or hotel executive to tamper with tradition can succeed. I am sure that we will continue to hear about ladies from all over the country who come to New York City and eat at the Waldorf Astoria, where they are served "Red Velvet Cake" *with* cocoa or chocolate and *without* any red coloring in the frosting; they will then be charged outrageous amounts of money for the simple secret formula. Finally, they will go back home to Detroit or Dubuque and tell all their friends about it and give away thousands of copies of the recipe along with uncounted slices of the crimson cake.

"The Snake in the Blanket"

In late 1968 and early 1969 a number of traditional themes in modern American folklore merged to create a new urban legend. The legend quickly spread by word of mouth from east to west, aided by frequent newspaper stories and mentions on radio programs. Its life span was remarkably short, however, as it had faded into relative obscurity by the early 1970s. The two basic elements, both familiar from other legends, were a business establishment, specifically a suburban discount store, and a dangerous creature discovered in an unexpected place. In the typical form of this legend a poisonous snake strikes an unaware shopper who is looking at some imported rugs or blankets. As usual, the constituent elements of the story (snake/blanket/foreign source/name of store/outcome) vary widely from version to version.

In 1969 a student at the State University College at Buffalo gave an account of "The Snake in the Blanket" as a rather flexible rumor from upstate New York. She reported it as circulating there as much as two years earlier (although such unverified datings are always suspect in folklore research):

> I live in a northern New York community, Pulaski, New York, which is about forty miles north of Syracuse. For the past two years a story has been circulating throughout the town about the unfortunate happening of a middle-aged woman who lived somewhere near our village. The woman or her home have never been identified. This is the story as I heard it, and ultimately believed it until recently.
>
> During the summer about two years ago my mother, a forty-nine year old housewife, was telling to everyone the news about a woman who was shopping in Weston's [a large bargain center which sells groceries, clothing, housewares and about everything, located in Watertown, New York, about thirty miles north of Pulaski], and looking at some woven rugs which were imported from a foreign country. The country was never really definitely identified, as I recall, but I know the country was not in Europe, but more like a country in the Far East. As I have heard the story retold I can remember countries like Japan, India, and China mentioned. While examining the rug, the woman in question put her hand inside a rolled up rug, suddenly had some kind of attack, and fell to the floor. The woman was rushed to a hospital but she was

dead when she arrived. The rug was unrolled at the store and inside there were a large poisonous snake [its type is not identified], and a few freshly hatched baby snakes. The woman had been bitten by this snake. As the story concludes, Weston's is faced with a whopping law suit, filed by the family of the deceased, and subsequently a lively discussion ensues about how the teller and listener of the story are never going to shop at Weston's again.

Students of folklorist Patrick B. Mullen in Buffalo contributed twenty-three variants of the legend in 1969, including the following typical, localized treatment:

> I first heard the story of the snake found in a blanket sometime during the month of February. I understand the story to be that a woman was feeling the texture of the blanket by sticking her hand in the folded pile of blankets that were on sale at Two Guys on Walden Avenue in Buffalo. She was bitten by a snake that was curled up in there. The woman died and the blankets were all shipped back to Hong Kong from where they had come. I heard from a friend the story was on radio, but denied in print in the newspaper.

Other Buffalo students said the blankets (or rugs, "woven straw rugs," dry goods . . .) had come from Pakistan (or India, Korea, Japan . . .). A friend of one collector said his mother had attended the funeral of the woman bitten by the snake. One informant said she heard the story from a woman whose friend had her arm in a bandage from the snakebite and was suing the store in which the snake had bitten her. A couple of students specified an electric blanket, not a rug, as the snake's hiding place; the snakes either hatched or were activated by the warmth when the blanket was turned on. (The prick in the finger was at first interpreted as coming from a loose wire in the blanket.) One person said cobra eggs that hatched in a blanket had been laid by a snake living in a bunch of bananas that were shipped to the United States on the same boat as the blankets from an unspecified tropical port. Another student thought the incident had happened as early as 1964 in Erie, Pennsylvania, and several had read about it in a newspaper, or had spoken to someone else who said they had. Consistently in all versions is the implication of sloppy practices or lower-grade merchandise in discount stores.

A Buffalo newspaper report—the earliest press mention of the story so far discovered—appeared in the *Evening News* of February 5, 1969, in a reader service column called "Newspower." It began:

> Q—Why hasn't your paper printed the story about the snake that crawled out of some imported goods at a local store, and bit a lady customer? C. L., Orchard Park.
> A—Because it's not true. It's a no-no.
> This is one of those bizarre stories that have been making the rounds in recent weeks. It's completely without foundation. The hospitals where the woman was supposed to have been taken say it just never happened.
> Such a victim would have needed anti-snake serum; only the Buffalo Zoo has an ample stock handy, and it remains intact.
> The story grew as it was told—like any good story. It ultimately became a cobra and seven little ones, which made the passage here in an Oriental rug!

But so popular was the legend in Buffalo that later that year the *Evening News* mentioned it again. The column "Curran's Corner" for September 19, 1969, reported that "the cobra tale" was a rumor that had been all over New York City and Buffalo (baby cobras hatched in sweaters imported from India); the chief veterinarian of New York, however, was quoted as saying that he had heard of no such case.

A Buffalo student from the borough of Queens, New York City, reported a variant set in her hometown:

> Over the summer, during the end of June, my girl friend came over to the house and told me of a woman who had died in the department store near her house.

THE VANISHING HITCHHIKER

The woman had been looking at Persian rugs when all of a sudden she got very red in the face and fainted. When the ambulance came, she was dead. They found a small sting on her finger. Then they found a bug, either a fly or spider, embedded in the rug. Apparently while the woman had been feeling the texture of the rug with her hands, gliding it back and forth, the bug bit her. It was poisonous and so she died. The department store was Korvette's, further out on the Island. This had an effect on the people I know; my one aunt at the time had ordered a carpet but she cancelled the order. And in my mind alone, when I went shopping with my parents for carpeting, I wouldn't let them feel the texture, thinking of the woman who had died.

The legend was flourishing at about the same time in the Washington, D.C., area. A student of folklorist George Carey, for example, claimed in 1969:

> This happened to my girlfriend's sister-in-law. One day she was shopping at Klein's Department Store in Greenbelt [Maryland]. She saw some sweaters that were on sale and tried some on. She felt this prick on her arm but thought it was just the tag. Anyway, she continued shopping. Later in the day her arm started itching. It swelled up and got real red. By evening she felt faint. Her husband took her to the hospital where she was listed in serious or critical condition. They completely retraced her steps that day to try and find out what happened to her. Come to find out it was from that prick from the sweaters. The sweaters had been imported from Japan. Somehow a snake got into them and started a nest. The eggs had hatched and there were little tiny snakes in some of the sweaters.

The details in this text about the victim's symptoms and the methodical search for the cause would seem to lend it credibility. However, in 1969 the Maryland Folklore Archive already contained seven different versions of the story, including one in which the victim was "the wife of a man who works in my husband's office," and five in which the woman still lay in critical condition in an unnamed area hospital. Japan and Vietnam were also given as the sources of the snake-infested product, and two accounts specified the snake as being a cobra. In his book Carey also reported that when he used these snake stories in a university lecture as examples of the urban legend in process he was called a liar by a New York City student who insisted that it had actually happened at Macy's to "a friend of a friend of her mother's." On February 13, 1969, the Washington *Star* had reported on their careful check of police, store, and hospital records in a story headlined "No Snakes in Sweaters; the Tale is Just a Yarn." Ten days later the *Star* ran a follow-up to the story, inspired by many calls to the newspaper which, it was reported, had "increased in number—and in certitude" since the publication of the earlier denial. The *Star* tried to link the story with an earlier legend about snakes in an amusement park fun house boat ride, not an impossible connection since such stories do still circulate orally in various parts of the United States.

By May of 1969 "The Snake in the Blanket" had reached the Midwest; the creature was now almost always secreted in a sweater or other item of clothing rather than a blanket or rug. Folklore instructor Xenia E. Cord collected versions from her students in the Indiana University Extension in Kokomo and from the local press. A Kokomo student's version was as follows:

> A woman was looking through the blouses at K-Mart and stuck herself with a pin. At least that's what she thought. It hurt so she went on home. Later her hand started swelling so she called the doctor. He examined it and said she hadn't stuck it with a pin, but that it had been bitten by a snake. An investigation was held at the K-Mart and two snakes were found in with the blouses.

They discovered that the blouses had come over here from Hong Kong and that the snakes had apparently been in with the blouses.

The informant added that her mother had heard the story from a woman whose husband had been told it by a policeman who had gotten it directly from the actual policeman who had investigated the case. Two other Indiana versions collected by Cord also specified a K-Mart as the scene; one supposedly in Tennessee, and the other a local store in the garden section. One of the sources claimed that she had heard about the event occurring in Chicago, as reported in a Sunday *Chicago Tribune* (issue as yet unlocated).

In Indiana the K-Marts seemed to bear most of the blame for the supposed incident, so much so that the *Kokomo Tribune* of May 25, 1969, published a denial of the legend in the "City Beat Notebook," and the *New Albany* [Indiana] *Tribune* on May 21, 1969, reported at length on a "Snake Rumor Exterminated at Clarksville":

> Some local residents have heard stories of snakes at the K-Mart store on Highway 131, Clarksville, and are letting their anxieties be known to the management. The management in turn, is telling them that there are no snakes at K-Mart.
>
> According to K-Mart officials, there are no snakes on the premise, nor have there been any verbal or written complaints from customers. They report that no one has seen or been bitten by a snake while on the K-Mart property.
>
> According to Donald Dickenson, store manager, the rumors have been circulating for several weeks, but a definite origin has yet to be found.
>
> The rumors reportedly had the snakes in the women's wear, patio and garden departments. A thorough search has failed to turn up anything more than a timid-looking pair of worms in the garden department.
>
> Patrons of the store need not fear, for should a cus-

tomer be bitten by a snake somewhere else, he need only go to the sporting goods department where he can purchase a reasonably priced snakebite kit.

It is characteristic that the newspaper reporter wanted to establish "a definite origin" for the rumor, and that the department store manager conducted "a thorough search" for the legendary snake. But folklore does not work that way; of course, nothing was ever found. The reporter's witticism in the last paragraph probably only served to feed the rumor. In fact, the discussion of such oral legends in published or broadcast sources—even if only to refute them—almost invariably spreads the story and helps keep it alive. In Terre Haute, Indiana, for instance, folklorist Ronald Baker observed that "this story was mentioned on a very popular radio talk show, spreading the legend to a broad audience of local housewives. The assistant manager of the K-Mart said, 'Women would call all day asking, "Did you catch that snake yet?" Customers were always asking the cashiers about the snake in yard goods. . . . We had some women who refused to go back to the yard goods.' "

Other Midwestern reports of the snake story appeared in the Bloomington, Indiana, *Daily Herald Telephone* (December 1, 1969; snakes in clothing imported from Japan) and in Columbus, Ohio (March, 1970; oral report of Japanese krait snakes in a carpet). By early summer, as evidenced by the July 1, 1969, "Herb Bechtold's Round Robin" column in the *Sioux Falls* [South Dakota] *Argus Leader,* "The Snake in the Blanket" had migrated through the upper Midwest into the northern plains states:

STORY ABOUT WOMAN, SNAKES WIDESPREAD

You've no doubt heard the story about the woman who was shopping for blankets and was supposedly bitten by a poisonous tropical snake.

A reader called the Argus-Leader and asked why there has been nothing in the paper about it.

Because it isn't true.

According to the story that has been making the rounds, the woman's hand is supposed to have ballooned after she felt what she thought was a sharp pin in the blanket she was examining. A recheck of the blanket is supposed to have disclosed a "family of baby snakes."

Reports reaching the Argus-Leader had the woman being from Larchwood, Worthington and various other places. Different stores were mentioned in different versions of the story.

Oddly enough, the same thing is supposed to have happened in Rochester, Minn., Minneapolis, St. Paul; La Crosse and Madison, Wis., and several other places.

The matter was checked out in every community with negative results.

A story in the St. Paul newspaper said: "It is a wild, probably malicious but unfounded rumor currently making the rounds in the Twin Cities. The incident is reported to have happened at different locations . . . [the newspaper] checked with each of the stores and with police in the various communities. No one was bitten and no one died."

The suspicion that the rumor was "malicious" was mentioned in several other reports, and foul play was suspected by many discount store managers interviewed by the press, but, as with "The Kentucky Fried Rat" and other legends mentioning specific businesses, there is no evidence of any "planted" derogatory stories. In fact, probably a person would have a fairly tough time trying to put a rumor or legend into circulation, especially in trying to confine it to only certain business establishments.

"The Snake in the Blanket" is a cautionary tale for unwary consumers. It reflects popular distrust not only of "big business" —the large impersonal chain stores—but of the alien Orient as well. Together the East and the chain store let loose a venomous snake, one of the most feared and loathsome of creatures, heavy with symbolism in popular psychology. Some folklorists have even suggested that the highly active tradition of the story in the late 1960s at the height of the Vietnam War revealed an American fear of entanglements with the Orient. Whether that theory is convincing or not, "The Snake in the Blanket" did diminish in popularity almost as quickly and mysteriously as it arose.

A Texas report, a story in the *Dallas Morning News* of June 15, 1970, is worth quoting in full since it illustrates so well the futile circular quest for origins likely to confront anyone trying to track down an urban legend. In a significant local variation, which reflected Texas prejudices, the source of the infested goods was not the Far East but Mexico:

THERE WAS THIS SNAKE, SEE . . .

"I'd like some information," a male caller told the Dallas News City Desk some weeks ago.

It seems he'd heard about a woman who had gone to a local discount store to look at some fur coats imported from Mexico. When the woman put her hand in the coat pocket, she felt a sudden, sharp pain. A few minutes later her arm supposedly had started turning black and blue.

"Well," the man continued, "they rushed her to the hospital. It seems that pain was a snake in the coat pocket. The woman's arm had to be amputated."

The reporter said he'd check the story.

About that time a woman called with the same story, only she'd heard the woman died right in Presbyterian Hospital's emergency ward.

Presbyterian Hospital said it had no such case in record.

"My brother is a doctor," another caller explained. "He's on the staff at Baylor Hospital and he was present when they brought the woman in."

Baylor Hospital said it also had no such case on record. Neither did the police or the health department.

The doctor was questioned, he said it wasn't actually he who was present but a friend.

169

The friend explained he wasn't present either, he had just overheard two nurses talking about it.

After about 10 calls from other "interested" persons the fur coat turned into some material that had come in from India. A man gave the name of the insurance company which was handling the case.

The insurance man said it wasn't actually his company, but his next door neighbor's cousin's company.

The story spread through the city and seemed to be the main topic of conversation at cocktail parties and bridge games.

Finally a caller came up with the victim's name.

The News called and the "victim" answered the phone.

She said she had never been in better health. Someone must have had her confused with someone else, but she had heard the rumor. Only she heard the snake was found in a basket of fruit.

The neighbor's cousin's insurance company was located.

He said the only snake bite victim he knew of was his daughter and that had happened on a family hike the summer before.

The managers of the two discount stores most frequently mentioned in the rumor said the story is one that has been traveling across the country. Both noted that neither store even sells fur coats.

The doctor who was actually supposed to have performed the surgery said he was a pediatrician and never did surgery.

"But as long as I've got you on the phone," he explained, "I'd like to ask you about something else. It seems a story going around about a young girl who got blood poisoning from a certain kind of spray net that's on the market . . . !"

Two years later (February 1972) the Boise *Idaho Statesman* insisted that "There is just no truth to the intriguing rumor that a snake (would you believe a 'black asp'?) took a 6,200-mile journey from Taiwan to bite a Boise woman in a local department store, it was generally agreed Friday." The manager of a Boise K-Mart denied the report saying, "We've heard this rumor around here for several months." These tiny snakes, it was said, had been sewn into the sleeve linings of the coats.

This is the last media appearance of "The Snake in the Blanket/Sweater" legend I have seen, though other folklorists have reported a few new versions since 1970. Many people can still remember hearing the story (and probably assumed that it was true) in past years, but it seems to be fairly dormant for the moment.

NOTES

"Red Velvet Cake"

Other famous hotels have been the subjects of legend cycles, but nothing to match the Waldorf Astoria and its apocryphal "Red Velvet Cake." For more New York City hotel-lore see Moritz Jagendorf, "The Rich Lore of a Rich Hotel, The Plaza," in *New York Folklore Quarterly,* 9 (1953), 176–182.

The Oregon/California text of "Red Velvet Cake" is from Suzi Jones, *Oregon Folklore* (Eugene: University of Oregon and the Oregon Arts Commission, 1977), p. 108.

I surveyed the tradition of "Red Velvet Cake" as I then understood it in a note published in *Oregon Folklore Bulletin,* 2 (Winter-Spring, 1963), pp. 5–7. The University of Idaho text was brought to me by Carol Biegert Brown in Fall 1963. Several of the clippings mentioned in this chapter were sent to me by freelance food writer Cynthia Scheer.

Information from the Waldorf Astoria comes from letters signed by Lola Preiss and Frances Borden dated August 10, 1965, and July 24, 1979.

Donna Lou Morgan, Food Editor of the *Salt Lake Tribune,* shared information with me contributed by her readers in 1979.

A parody of Freudian analysis of folk legends using the "Red Velvet Cake" story as its example was published by Keith Cunningham in *Folklore Forum,* 5 (1972), 147–148. In his version, a $100 cake has a psychosexual relation to the novel *The Hundred*

Dollar Misunderstanding, among other things. This one must be read to be believed.

"The Snake in the Blanket"

The Buffalo, New York, texts of "The Snake in the Blanket" come from Patrick B. Mullen's article "Department Store Snakes" in *Indiana Folklore,* 3 (1970), 214–228. Mullen also mentioned an item on the story in the "Action Line" column of the *Houston Post,* June 30, 1970. In his article "Modern Legend and Rumor Theory," *Journal of the Folklore Institute,* 9 (1972), 95–109, Professor Mullen quoted the item from the Buffalo *Evening News,* February 5, 1969, on p. 101.

The Maryland texts and the Washington *Star's* article in February, 1969, were cited and partially quoted in George G. Carey, *Maryland Folk Legends and Folk Songs* (Cambridge, Maryland: Tidewater Publishers, 1971), pp. 74–75.

Xenia E. Cord published three oral texts of "The Snake in the Blanket" from Indiana and referred to newspaper reports in her note "Department Store Snakes" in *Indiana Folklore,* 2 (1969), 110–114. The story from the *New Albany Tribune,* May 21, 1969, quoted in this chapter appears on p. 113, and Cord described a photograph accompanying the article that shows a security guard with a sign denying that any snakes have been found on the store premises. She quoted another denial of the story that appeared in "Schull's Mailbag" in the *Indianapolis News,* May 23, 1969.

Ronald L. Baker described the incident in Terre Haute, Indiana, in his article "The Influence of Mass Culture on Modern Legends," *Southern Folklore Quarterly,* 40 (1976), 367–376; the quotation in this chapter is on page 371. "The Snake in the Blanket" was discussed in another article in the same issue of that journal: Donald Allport Bird, "A Theory for Folklore in Mass Media: Traditional Patterns in the Mass Media," *SFQ,* 40 (1976), 285–305 (see pages 293–294).

My colleague Robert Steensma provided the item from the *Sioux Falls Argus-Leader,* July 1, 1969.

The June 15, 1970, *Dallas Morning News* story was quoted in full in the "Folklore in the News" column of *Western Folklore,* 30 (1971), 141–142.

The *Idaho Statesman* clipping, undated except for month and year, and headlined "Store Denies Boise Woman Bitten by Snake

Inside Coat," was sent to me by Louie Attebery, The College of Idaho, Caldwell.

Ann Carpenter reported a recurrence of "The Snake in the Blanket" legend in Texas in 1974 in her article "Cobras at K-Mart: Legends of Hidden Danger," *Publications of the Texas Folklore Society,* 40 (1976), 36–45.

8 | Urban Legends in the Making

At the same time that the best-known urban legends are circulating among the public at large in well-wrought versions with countless variations of detail, other fragmentary rumors and stories are being told—sometimes only within a specific "folk group"—that interact with and borrow from the established legends. These undeveloped rumors and stories constitute a virtual floating anthology of possible urban legends in the making. While some are anonymous adaptations of older traditional motifs which come alive suddenly and briefly after years of inactivity, others may have a sustained local or regional popularity but never catch on with the general public, usually because they are too much the esoteric cultural possession of a particular ethnic or occupational group. Occasionally one of these "proto-legends" (rumors, beliefs, etc.) surfaces in the media but does not become widely known in oral tradition except as a conversational reference to a news report.

"The Economical Car"

A typical example of a recurrent rumor manifesting itself sometimes as a full-fledged narrative is the old urban tradition of an amazingly economical car (most often with a carburetor that can burn water). This story has run rampant for a short time repeatedly in the last thirty years, only to fade away again as the modern technical miracle fails to appear. "The Economical Car" shares with other urban legends the themes of remarkable automobile experiences and business ripoffs, but only infrequently is it collected in multiple examples with full narrative development. More often it is merely a brief report of a supposed incident, lacking verifying details. Given the rocketing gasoline prices in the past decade, it is not surprising that stories of "The Economical Car" have recently been circulating anew. An item in the *AP Log* for 18 September, 1978, gave few details about the car but described at length one Associated Press reporter's frustration in trying to trace its source:

BIG CAR STORY GETS DOWN-SIZED

It started with a tip from the brother-in-law of an AP staffer—and it sounded like it would be the story-of-the-year:

A Ford dealer had somehow mistakenly sold to a woman customer an experimental car which ran 1,000 miles on a tank of fuel. The tip even included her name and telephone number.

The situation had been revealed, the tip said, when she brought the car in for routine servicing. Allegedly, the buyer was to get $30,000 to return the car and keep the whole thing a secret. . . .

So, Malcolm Carter of the national staff in New York called the telephone number, which turned out to be the woman's office. But she had left for the day. Happily, her home number was listed. Unhappily, there was no answer.

After repeated efforts, however, he reached her. "Vowing that I would go to jail before divulging her name, I edged into my questioning. She sounded as if she didn't know what I was talking about at first, thereby convincing me that I was hot on the trail."

Carter mentioned the car.

No, she said, she didn't have such a car. But she dimly recollected a conversation many months ago with her insurance agent. One of his clients, she said, had told him about the miracle car.

The woman told Carter she would call the agent and then call back. "Someone ought to tell the story. It was outrageous," she said.

"When she called back, she said the insurance agent was eager for me to do the story. But the car didn't belong to his client. However, a friend of his client knew about it. She said he was trying to find out more for me and volunteered his number. Although I was growing increasingly skeptical, I was determined to get to the bottom of the story.

"I contacted the agent. He confirmed that he had talked to his client's friend and she didn't own the car. However, she had heard about it and was trying to track it down.

"Could I talk to her?" I ventured. "Why not?" he replied.

Carter then called the friend of the client of the agent of the first woman.

A baby-sitter answered. She didn't know when the mother would be home from work, didn't know her business number and didn't know when the husband would return.

But Carter kept calling and finally got the husband. "Oh yes," he replied. He had heard about the car.

Where? From who?

Well, he and his wife were in a bar one night when some guy said he had heard that some woman had a car that . . .

The anti big-business tone of this story, of course, is familiar to students of urban legends, especially when combined as it is here (also in "The Kentucky Fried Rat" and other such

177

tales) with an attempt to pay off and silence a consumer. The automobile manufacturer, evidently, wants to suppress the super car in order to protect oil company profits. The endless chain of informants, as we have repeatedly observed, is another hallmark of legendary material, while the theme of a mystery-car—so well known in other legends—is almost enough to discredit the story from the start, if the 1000 miles per tank figure did not already. The well-known fraudulence of nearly all gas-saving gadgets should also help to debunk this story.

Mint-Condition Vintage Vehicles

If it isn't a miraculous new car, it is sure to be an old one, preferably a vintage model, that legends tell of. Time and again we hear of the lost forgotten boxcar in a desert town's switching yard that is packed full of decades-old Ford Model-A's that never drove a mile beyond the factory gate. (Did they even ship Fords by freight train in the late 1920s?) Or you may hear something like this from a motorcycle fanatic:

> My friend Rusty in 1968 heard from a friend of a friend that it was possible to buy World War II vintage Harley-Davidson motorcycles for $25.00 if you bought them in lots of fifty. He went to the Salt Lake Army surplus store and the man there referred him to the Bountiful Army surplus store since he knew nothing about it. The man who ran the store in Bountiful said that he was on every mailing list for Army surplus sales in the United States and that he had never seen such an offer for Harley-Davidson motorcycles. He stopped looking, since that seemed rather final, but three years later he heard the same story from a man who lived in Moab, Utah.

Ghost Truckers and "The Ghost Airliner"

Folklore has lost no time in weaving legends around some of the newest heroes of popular culture—truckdrivers. There are ghostly truckers, who never quite manage to replace the earlier ghostly hitchhikers, but who roll on night after night like eighteen-wheel diesel Flying Dutchmen. Other legendary truckers trim a hippie's long hair using a handy pair of scissors (standard truck equipment?), or else they drive over and neatly squash the motorcycles of some tough punks who park in front of truck stops in order to hassle the hard-working, straight-arrow drivers.

One of the most interesting supernatural legends of today's transportation is "The Ghost Airliner" of Eastern Airlines (at least Eastern is frequently reported as the "source" of the tradition). Folklorist Richard C. Poulsen summed up the first version he received of this story (1974) from a correspondence course student in folklore who was an airline stewardess:

> . . . a jetliner had crashed somewhere in America. A number of people were killed, including the captain and other crew members. Because the plane was not totally destroyed, the airline . . . decided to rebuild the plane. Soon the aircraft was restored to service, but shortly after, a series of mysterious events cropped up around this particular plane.
>
> Both passengers and crew began hearing strange noises during flight. Some of these noises were voices of people who had died in the earlier crash. Before long, flight personnel became hesitant to travel on that particular plane, and the mysterious noises continued. The airline tried to sell the plane, without success, and finally it was taken out of service [and is] now standing abandoned in a lonely hangar somewhere in the United States.

In a series of interviews in 1975 and 1976 Poulsen found several other airline employees who knew the story, some having learned it during flight training; several firmly denied any element of truth to it. Still, Poulsen says, he gained "the distinct impression that talking about such things while in flight was not wise," and he collected this nicely-detailed version from one Texas International flight attendant:

179

There was this father and daughter who both worked for Eastern. He was a pilot—captain or something, I think—and she was a stewardess. He was flying a DC-8 or DC-10 or something, I can't remember, but he crashed the plane and was killed. Well, his daughter kept on flying and on one trip (on the same kind of aircraft her father was killed on) her father's ghost appeared to her and told her the wiring in the plane was faulty, and sure enough, when they checked there was a fire in the wiring. They say that he appeared to her when she opened the door of a warmer oven—his face was there. He appeared to other people on that same kind of aircraft and told them that that kind of plane was unsafe.

"The Devil in the Dancehall"

Even more bizarre than a ghost on an airliner is "The Devil in the Dancehall," another old and traditional, legend-theme now updated. Many Mexican and Spanish-American legends tell of a person who encounters witches or other diabolical beings dancing in a ghastly fiesta, with feet like horse's hooves or chicken claws. Some recent versions are set in Latin nightclubs in the contemporary southwest. As *Texas Monthly* reports it, the Devil appears like this:

> Dressed as a dashing *vaquero,* [cowboy] he finds the young woman who is playing hardest to get, then steals her heart away on the dance floor to the beat of a polka. It is *Love Story* revisited—until the chosen lady notices that her talented partner has chicken's feet, a typical sign of the Devil. The poor *señorita* emits a few screams of *"¡Sus pies! ¡Sus Pies!"* before she faints. But it is too late. Once revealed, the Devil disappears into the men's room, leaving behind a cloud of smoke, the smell of sulphur, and some great dance steps.

Next, I suppose, we could hear of "The Devil in a Disco" if this Hispanic tradition should enter Anglo folklore. The appearance of the story—along with a very flashy illustration—in *Texas Monthly* may already have effected such a transfer of lore.

Hilarious Accidents

What I call "hilarious accident stories" seem to include another emerging theme in urban legends. I have heard four distinct treatments of it so far. Two of them involve patients who are newly admitted to a hospital, or sometimes they meet in the emergency room. Their conversation concerns "What happened to you?" In the first variation each patient tries to top the other with the story of his injury; the first had blown himself off the toilet by flipping a lighted cigarette down the bowl, not realizing his wife had just squirted in some hair spray to kill a spider moments before he sat down; the second patient was using a rope tied around his waist, tossed up over the house, and tied to the car's rear bumper in order to be hoisted up to fix the television antenna (or to shovel snow off his roof), when his wife jumped behind the wheel and headed for the beauty parlor. (Notice in both stories how it is the wife who is principally at fault.) The patients in the third hilarious accident story are a male and female skier just brought down from the slopes on stretchers. She admits that her accident happened when she sneaked behind a pine tree in order to urinate without getting out of her ski bindings; she got her pants down (partial nudity again), but then her skis slipped, and down the hill she went, out of control. And *his* accident? Well, he saw this bare-bottomed woman ski by and he laughed so hard that he collided with a ski-lift tower. All of these accident stories also occur independently of the hospital setting, and there are several variations circulating on the toilet-seat and house-repair injuries. The fourth accident story —not quite so hilarious—provides only the visual evidence of an injury, though the preceding accident is obvious. A camper-trailer owner has converted his spare gas tank into a holding tank for the camper toilet. One morning he comes out and finds a siphon hose on the ground next to the vehicle, and alongside it is clear evidence that some would-be gasoline thief has been very, very sick. Among other accident legends in the making recently are stories involving butane cigarette-lighters, superglue, and "cruise control" on family cars or campers.

Kidnappings

No matter how credible, local, and thoroughly non-traditional an odd rumor or story seems to be, its true folk character may finally become clear when it is investigated closely. This was brought home to me sharply in the summer session of 1978 when several students in my American Folklore class reported the kidnapping of a small child during a family outing at Lagoon, a large amusement park in Farmington, just north of Salt Lake City. I had not seen any news report on the case, but it seemed quite believable that an infant or child could be snatched from the usually crowded park and whisked away via the nearby freeway. Mormon congregations often enjoy summer "Lagoon Day" outings to the park, and the families are large and well distributed by ages. Parents and older siblings could easily lose track of a baby or toddler, and tourists or strangers—perhaps criminal types—might well be lurking about such places (although Lagoon is a very wholesome amusement park). True, there were a few variations in the story: some said the child had been abducted by black people, while others heard it was a black-market adoption ring. And then I heard that it was really an older child who was taken, and that she (seldom "he") had been recognized later (by whom?) as an actor in a kiddy-porn film.

A couple of students became interested in the story and asked more questions. It turned out that some Utah informants associated the kidnapping with Disneyland rather than Lagoon, but they believed that it was still a Utah Mormon family on vacation in California that suffered the tragic loss of their child. One especially enterprising student telephoned several newspapers in and around Anaheim, California, and learned that the story was indeed known there, but since no evidence of such a crime had been uncovered, no newspaper had used the story. Disneyland officials denied the tale.

Within a month a Salt Lake City television station (KSL-TV) got wind of the rumor and made a thorough investigation, even attempting to trace the tradition back from one informant to another. Eventually they located a man who had been told "Disneyland" but who retold the story as "Lagoon," and one Mormon ward [congregational] newsletter had published the rumor as a warning to its members to watch their children very closely if they visited Lagoon. The Lagoon owners, of course, took pains to explain that no such crime had ever occurred at their park. One local person interviewed for the television feature said that whether the story was true or not, it still carried an important warning message to parents of small children, an extremely perceptive remark on the function of this folk tradition. A sociologist from Brigham Young University in Provo commented that for Mormons such a story served to explain by what means there could be such horrible things in God's good world as kiddy-porn and black-market adoption rings. Evil outsiders were the cause, or so the story implied, and even pious folk were never completely safe.

Delighted with the apparent unraveling of the local story as a transplant from the California original to Utah, probably facilitated by the popularity of Disneyland vacations among Utah Mormons and suspicions about Californians among many Utahans, I borrowed a videotape of the KSL-TV report and showed it at the annual meeting of the American Folklore Society in Salt Lake City in October, 1978. Confident that I was sharing with my fellow folklorists a true instance of the birth of a local urban legend, I was surprised to be told by conference attendees from several midwestern and eastern states that in fact virtually the same story was current—and had been for up to two years—in amusement parks, beaches, and other recreational areas in their own states. Furthermore, a similar story was going around now about a teenager who was nearly abducted while she was shopping in a department store or suburban mall; her attempted captor had managed to drug her, and he was just making his getaway when her parents or a store detective arrived for the rescue.

Well, whether we had an original Utah legend on our hands or not, this was all grist for the mill, so I gave the new versions from the wider tradition to my next folklore class as examples of the legend process still working its familiar magic. Then the hands went up: "Oh no! That *really* happened here in Salt Lake City. It was in the Auerbach's [a department store] parking garage, and this girl's mother waited and waited for the girl to join her in the car. She finally went in to look for her, and she got there just barely in time to stop this really sinister guy who had a cloth with a sedative of some kind over her mouth and nose and was leading her away. I read it in the paper . . . or heard it on the radio . . . or something."

Clearly, this was one more instance of an urban legend in the making.

NOTES

A copy of the *AP Log* for September 18, 1978, containing "The Economical Car" story that is quoted in this chapter on page four, was sent to me by Lynn Packer of KSL-TV. I am also grateful to Mr. Packer for a videotape of his excellent feature on the kidnappings at Lagoon or Disneyland story as it was broadcast locally in late summer, 1978.

The story about the vintage Harley-Davidson motorcycles for sale cheaply was collected by Kathy Reeder, a student of mine in Fall Quarter, 1971; she heard it from Rusty Flow of Salt Lake City.

Ronald L. Baker discussed recent trucker legends on pages 374 to 375 of his article "The Influence of Mass Culture on Modern Legends," *Southern Folklore Quarterly*, 40 (1976), 367–376.

Richard C. Poulsen documented "The Ghost Ship: A Legend Among Airline Personnel" in *Indiana Folklore*, 9 (1978), 63–69. He collected much of his material while en route to and from the 1975 annual meeting of the American Folklore Society in New Orleans.

"The Devil in the Dancehall" as I quote it is from an article titled "GGGhost Stories" by Joe Nick Patoski in *Texas Monthly* (October, 1978), 134–139. A traditional version from south of the border appeared in Américo Paredes, ed., *Folktales of Mexico* (Chicago: University of Chicago Press, 1970), pp. 25–26. Paredes cited motifs G216.1. *Witch with goose (chicken) feet,* and G303.4.5.3.1. *Devil detected by his hoofs.*

The hilarious accident stories come from late 1978 and early 1979. A story circulated by the Reuter News Agency, datelined Cape Town, described an accident involving a man on a roof with a rope around his waist tied to the bumper of his car which was driven away by his wife; it was published in the *Salt Lake Tribune* on 6 January 1980. The Lagoon Kidnapping story faded out in late summer or early fall of 1978, and it was not revived, to my knowledge, in summer 1979, although the kidnapping story attached to a local department store is still circulating.

Afterword

The succession of popular themes in American urban legends serves as a rough index of people's concerns and fantasies as they have changed through time. Probably even "The Vanishing Hitchhiker"—superb ghost story that it is—would not have enjoyed its continued appeal if the vehicle had not been changed from the horses and buggies found in nineteenth-century prototypes of this legend to the modern automobile. Our great esteem for cars and their relatively high cost have also contributed to the popularity of "The Death Car." The separate idea of marital infidelity (another sure winner) enters such later car-legends as "The Philanderer's Porsche" and "The Solid Cement Cadillac." But even more significant than the automobile's mere presence, since at least the 1950s we find references in urban legends to the *social* effects of living in a youth-oriented, mobile, car-loving society. This is clearly shown in such folk narratives as "The Hook," "The Boyfriend's Death," and "The Killer in the Backseat," all of which incorporate the young-driver, the defenseless-female, and the fearsome-stranger themes so typical of the accident reports and crime stories regularly encountered in the media.

Our data are incomplete in many respects, but if a preliminary history of American urban legends is sketched out we would have to say that from the turn of the century to World War II only the death/ghost/car stories really seemed to thrive. A few other legends that emerged full-blown and vigorous later were just beginning to appear then; these include "The Dead Cat in the Package" (1906?), "The Nude Surprise Party" (1927), and "Alligators in the Sewers" (1935) and "The Runaway Grandmother" (late 1930s). Following the war, we find that both "The Death Car" and "The Dead Cat in the Package" had reached Europe, while "The Runaway Grandmother" was firmly established in American tradition, evidently from a European wartime source. Popular teenage stories like "The Spider in the Hairdo" and "The Hook" appeared by the mid-1950s, as did the more sedate and domestically-appealing "Red Velvet Cake" story. Recreational vehicles entered legends at about the same period, and some inner-city legends began to migrate, as families were then doing, to the suburbs with their commuters and shopping malls.

All of the earlier urban legends continued to circulate through the 1960s along with further new variations on horror plots ("The Boyfriend's Death," "The Killer in the Backseat," etc.), and at the end of the decade there was a proliferation of imported "Snakes in Blankets" and of marijuana growing along with the alligators down in the sewers of New York City and occasionally elsewhere. Early in the 1970s the decades-old motif of foreign matter in food suddenly blossomed in "The Kentucky Fried Rat" story along with the European counterpart ("Rat Bone in the Chicken Salad," etc.); the cement-filled car had found its way to Europe as well, although in a variant form. The latest technical gadgets and cultural trends—such as to microwave cooking and disco dancing—are reflected in current urban legends, but at the same time traditional ghostly vehicles (now airliners) and ghostly hitchhikers (now Jesus or one of His followers) keep appearing. If there is a lesson in all of this, it may be that whatever is new and puzzling or scary, but which eventually becomes familiar, may turn up in modern folklore.

In a general way our urban legends often depict a clash between modern conditions and some aspect of a traditional lifestyle. For example, keeping a pet is something of an anachronism in urban housing with working family-members, and the *dead* pet from an apartment poses an especially uncomfortable problem of disposal. Similarly, an aged grandmother may be regarded as a nuisance by Americans nowadays, especially (in the nightmarish legend) when she dies on a vacation trip abroad. Since we believe we should not have to deal directly with such things as death any more (and actually we seldom do), the folk stories adopt the culturally acceptable solution to such problems in the arrival of a helpful anonymous stranger, whether shoplifter, thief, or mortician. (Remember that in some earlier versions of "The Vanishing Hitchhiker," taking a corpse into the car was an acceptable motif to storytellers; but now the first response to the body is to get it out on the roof, and then to get rid of it for good as soon as possible.)

Children, once mostly reared by their parents, are now often left in the care of strangers; thereby they may be endangered, legends assert, along with the baby-sitters themselves. Microwave ovens and mind-expanding drugs may come together to produce tragic results; better, perhaps, say the urban legends, if we had stuck with conventional ovens and old-fashioned stimulants. (It is conveniently forgotten that tipsy baby-sitters also crammed babies into gas or electric ovens in the older folklore.) In our new, mobile lifestyle (bound to change as energy costs continue to rise) even someone trying to feel at-home-on-the-road in his own camper or trailer is clearly in the wrong element, and so he must suffer a naked warning shock before he gets safely home and into his clothes again. Hairsprays, airliners, Cokes, and Big Macs are fraught with gruesome dangers—spiders, ghosts, rodents, and worms, respectively. The shopping-center discount stores, those most characteristic modern marketing centers, continue to retain vestiges of the lack of quality control and standardization typical of earlier American commerce, except that now the flawed products are imported from backward countries.

The distrust of foreigners runs deep in other aspects of modern folklore (such as ethnic slurs and dialect jokes), but urban legends emphasize instead the shortcomings of some of our own institutions, such as large hotels, manufacturers, food processors, department stores, and fast-food restaurants. These are held up to scrutiny and criticism in the legends, and they are found wanting. When the consumer finally manages to win a case against the company lawyers, he or she is alleged to have gained large monetary judgments; but the dollar figures are always much greater in folklore than in real life, just as the car bargains are mostly legendary rather than objectively provable.

For all the threats and injuries coming from outside sources in the urban legends, many of the crises they deal with are simply the result of normal human misjudgment and poor luck. Time and again the meanings of stories are clear: "He should have known better," "She got what she deserved," etc. The girlfriend, baby-sitter, or roommate, for example, should not have been left alone, and even when she was she might have asserted herself and have given some life-saving help. The boss ought never to have assumed that everyone in his family forgot his birthday and that his beautiful secretary was really ready to jump into bed with him. The cement truck driver should have stayed on the job and trusted his wife. The nude rider in the trailer should not have been there like that in the first place, or at least he should have stayed there. The middle-aged female shoplifter and the foreign car-thieves merely get to keep what they unluckily stole—a dead cat and a dead body. Just about the only *innocent* victims we find in these stories seem to be the baby in the oven (although at least one of them is put there because he cries too much) and the snake-bitten woman shopper (although maybe she should have had the sense to shop elsewhere).

It is tempting to take one or two of the most typical recent American urban legends as inclusive symbols of distinctive aspects of our recent history. "The Snake in the Blanket," some have suggested, reflects our guilt stemming from the war in Vietnam, and implies that the venomous intentions we fear that some Asian peoples may feel toward us in the postwar period are manifesting themselves in revenge via imported goods. If we follow this line of interpretation, we might say that "The Baby in the Oven" develops from suppressed desires to commit infanticide, represents mixed love and hate for our children, guilt for sometimes leaving them with strangers, dread of extermination by modern technology, and deep-seated distrust of outsiders coming into our homes.

Without denying that such themes are implied in these tales, or that legends are generally appealing at more than one level, I believe that a great deal of their continuing popularity can be explained more simply in terms of an artistic exploration in oral tradition of the *possibilities* of things. Goods are imported in quantity from some countries with tropical climates: *what if* a snake or snake eggs got into them (as insects sometimes stow away in fruit shipments)? Microwave ovens are becoming more common in homes all the time: *what if* a living creature got into one (as a cat sometimes climbs into a warm clothes-drier left open)? As in any age or with any subject—when a skilled storyteller begins to play with such ideas, and when members of his audience respond, repeat the stories, and begin to add their own flourishes, then legends begin to form and to circulate. Probably by the time this is being read new examples of false-true tales will already be going around, and these urban legends too will contain symbols of our culture and reflections of our lives.

Glossary of Terms
in Urban Legend Study

communal re-creation. The process by which oral folklore varies as it is passed from person to person in a folk group. Often no single individual may be credited with changes, but each member of the group who repeats an item contributes to its variation or "re-creation." (A theory developed in ballad studies but applicable to narratives as well.)

fairy tale. A common term for fictional folktales, mostly European, involving heroes, tasks, magic, rewards, etc., and set in an unspecified time and place: "Once upon a time. . . ." Folklorists prefer to call these stories (such as "Cinderella") "wonder tales," or, following German usage, "*Märchen.*"

folklore. ". . . those materials in culture that circulate traditionally among members of any group in different versions, whether in oral form or by means of customary example, as well as the processes of traditional performance and communication." (Jan Harold Brunvand, *The Study of American Folklore: An Introduction*, 2nd. edn. [New York: W. W. Norton, 1978], p. 7.)

folktale. The general term for fictional folk narratives (fairy tale, joke, tall tale, etc.) as opposed to myths and legends, which are believed, or at least told as if true. "Tale" and "story," however, are often used, even by folklorists, in the general sense of any folk narrative.

informant. The human source from whom folklore is collected: storyteller, singer, folk healer, craftsman, etc.

joke. A humorous fictional folktale that is relatively short (usually one major episode, though sometimes repeated) and ends with a punch line.

legend. Folk narratives that deal with realistic incidents set in the past. Though they are told as "true" stories—and are often believed—legends sometimes contain supernatural and bizarre elements.

motif. A traditional narrative unit—such as a character, object, or action—that serves as a building block of folk stories of all kinds. Many older motifs are cataloged in Stith Thompson's six-volume work *The Motif-Index of Folk Literature* (Copenhagen and Bloomington: Indiana University Press, 1955–1958). Newer kinds of folk narrative, such as urban legends, generate their own characteristic motifs which are not yet cataloged. (A ghost is a traditional motif, and a maniac with a hook in place of a hand is a modern one.)

oral tradition. The process of word-of-mouth transmission by which verbal folklore is disseminated, person to person and generation to generation. By extension, oral tradition is also sometimes used with reference to the customary transmission of behavioral and material folk tradition.

proto-legend. Raw material for a possible future legend in the form of a rumor or a folk belief.

rumor. A brief, anonymous, unverified report of a supposed event that circulates both by word of mouth and in the mass media. Rumors tend to be relatively short-lived and non-narrative as contrasted to legends, though rumors may contribute to legend growth and spread.

subtype. A group of folk narrative texts with distinctively developed plots that still share basic plot features in common with other subtypes of a larger general pattern of narrative. For example, one subtype of "The Dead Cat" legend involves theft of the pet's corpse; another one describes the substitution of a piece of meat for the corpse. (See also "variant.")

theme. In folk narratives, a general topic, such as food contamination or nudity, that is characteristic of a given tale or legend cycle. Usually "theme" is used for elements larger than a "motif" and can refer to a particular message, viewpoint, or attitude.

variant. Used both for any text of a folk narrative (or other kind of oral lore) and for a distinctively developed group of texts (i.e., a "subtype"). Most folklorists do not distinguish between "variant," "version," and "text," using these terms interchangeably.

APPENDIX

Collecting and Studying Urban Legends

Urban legends offer an unusual opportunity for amateur folk-lorists to do original and valuable research in American folk-lore, since, as this book demonstrates, much of our information on these legends has come from student collectors or the accidental discoveries of legends in the mass media. As in any folklore research, the basic steps of collection, classification, and analysis are involved, and a brief review of these steps with special attention to urban legends is sufficient for a beginning scholar. Those desiring more detailed guidance should read my general textbook, *The Study of American Folklore*, 2nd. edn. (New York: W. W. Norton, 1978), and my anthology of sample studies, *Readings in American Folklore* (New York: W. W. Norton, 1979).

As a typical genre of modern folklore, urban legends are known to many Americans in a wide range of ages and backgrounds, but particularly middle-class urban and small-town people who are reasonably aware of the news and current events. You will not need to travel to the backwoods or seek out "folksy" informants to collect urban legends; in fact, it would be a fine idea to begin by writing down those that you and your family and friends already know. What variations have you heard of the urban legends discussed in this book? What other stories—possibly urban legends—have you heard?

Ideally—as with all folklore—urban legends should be collected in natural social situations with the least possible interference from the collector, and with maximum data recorded about the oral performance. You can collect in your own school or church group or at Scout meetings, campouts, slumber parties, or cocktail parties. Instead of simply waiting for people to tell you urban legends, you can encourage an "induced natural context" by bringing up the subject in a conversational situation and then subtly urging people to tell the stories they know. Once such a narrating group is established, it is usually not necessary for the collector to take much part in the conversation. You should concentrate on writing down or recording the stories, noting facial expressions, gestures, audience reaction, and other subjects of conversation. It would be interesting to include people from different regions or even different countries in such a group in order to see if varying forms of the standard urban legends will be introduced. The essential facts about each storyteller should be secured: name, age, sex, level of education, and where the story was learned.

The collected texts must be recorded accurately in a notebook or with a tape recorder, and the taped examples must be transcribed literally. In addition to transcribing verbatim texts of urban legends, you should also record other information which will help you to analyze them. For example, what comments can you elicit from storytellers as to the truth or possible meaning of their legends? (Ask, "Do you believe this story?" and "What do you suppose this story means?") Are informants aware of other versions? Have they ever seen such stories in print, and can they remember approximately where and when? What is their reaction to the idea that these are "just legends?" (It is best to avoid calling them "folklore" or "legend" when first collecting, but the question of belief could be introduced when discussing the stories later.)

One interesting collecting technique is to follow a chain of legend transmission from person to person back several steps. From whom did your informant hear a particular legend, and from whom did that source hear it? A string of several legend texts collected in this way should exhibit the effects of "communal re-creation," that is, the making of variants in oral transmission. Another project might be to invent a rumor or legend similar to an actual urban legend and then to tell it to a friend, and see whether it catches on in tradition and spawns variants. Or you might arrange (without your informants knowing it) for one legend teller to narrate his or her version in the presence of another person who knows the same legend. Then you could observe the reaction of the listener, and later you might collect the listener's version once again in order to determine whether there has been any influence from the first narrator.

If possible, references to mass media appearances of urban legends should be traced to a source, but do not be overly disappointed if this proves to be impossible. Ask your informants whether they can find copies of the printed sources they have seen, or try to determine their dates so you can search for them in library files of magazines or newspapers. If the source was a local newspaper, the paper's editors and reporters may be willing to help find the published story, or they may want to write up some legends you have collected as a news item. (Such articles may be the source of further texts, either through letters to the editor or through readers contacting you about the stories you are interested in.) There is no practical way to search systematically for media examples of urban legends in general, but if you happen to see one in the press, be sure to clip or copy it, and note the source, date, and page. If you collect legends about local businesses, you may want to inverview the owners or managers of these businesses to see if they are aware of the stories and of any possible effects on sales.

The classification of the legends you collect will partly be a matter of matching them to the examples given in this book, which represent the major American urban legends previously identified by folklorists. Although new urban legends will eventually spring up, for the most part you are likely to hear those that are discussed here. But surely you will encounter interesting subtypes and variations on these stories—changes in plot details that signify a true living oral folk tradition. By identifying the general themes and patterns in your collected texts, as is done repeatedly in this book, you can sort out the basic story types and then distinguish the local variations. Which themes are the most popular in your collection: ghosts, horrors, business ripoffs, nudity . . . ? As your collection grows, you will probably want to look up some of the scholarly articles on urban legends cited in the notes to this book, if you live near a library large enough to contain some of the major folklore journals.

Whether you have access to the folkloristic literature or not, some analysis of your legends is possible just by following the principles discussed and demonstrated in this book. (See especially pp. 13–16.) One good possibility is to compare the local cycles of urban legends with the more widespread traditions described and summarized here. Exactly how are your region's legends adapted to their setting? What details are included to support their air of veracity? How are they linked to other local legends or to specific sites in the area? If you discover a new subtype, what does it reveal about changing attitudes or preferences in the community? Do the structural patterns in your texts conform generally to those in this book, and, if not, what do the variations suggest symbolically?

Another interesting question is the extent to which your informants will accept the meanings which folklore scholars have identified in urban legend studies. For example, do only young women in your community tell "The Boyfriend's Death" and "The Hook," or do young men tell them too? Do the tellers regard these as true stories? What do they feel are their most significant warnings or messages? What "morals" do people draw from "The Snake in the Blanket," "Red Velvet Cake," or "The Kentucky Fried Rat"? How do your informants react to the suggested meanings said to underly a story like "The Runaway Grandmother"? Does your community have a particular cultural slant—say, ultra-conservatism or an ethnic component—that is reflected in the most popular urban legends or legend subtypes?

Style in legend-telling is something you can study from the data easily collected from local narrators. If you know a particularly gifted narrator, or one who knows several urban legends, collect a number of different tellings of each one before different audiences, and take notes on how each performance is enlivened by vocal or gestural effects, perhaps influenced by the audiences' reception of the tales. What seems to be the function of each legend, and how does the style help to support this? By what means does the storyteller assert the truth of the legends that he or she tells?

Teachers not only have an especially good opportunity to hear and collect urban legends—if they can gain the confidence of their students to talk about such "non-educational" matters—but they can also use urban legend studies as class projects. For example, if a whole class were to collect and compare local examples of urban legends they could put together an anthology of typical versions from their community and study the ways in which they have been localized. Over a period of time it would be interesting to see how the legends of a school have grown and changed.

Any American folklorist would be grateful for information about what you find in your urban legend studies in order to see how our present understanding of legend growth and development has been expanded by your research. If you live near a college or university with a folklorist on the staff, by all means share your findings with him or her. Most folklorists (or their institutions) maintain archives of collected material where you can deposit your texts and find other texts for comparison. But whether you can meet another folklorist or not, I for one would be most interested in your urban legend research. Please write to me at this address:

> Professor Jan Harold Brunvand
> Department of English
> University of Utah
> Salt Lake City, Utah 84112

Index

Index